CONTENTS

q 16.00

A Practical Guide to
Intensive Interaction

MELANIE NIND & DAVID HEWETT

371.9 NIN

British Institute of Learning Disabilities

ACKNOWLEDGEMENTS

We are very grateful to our extended network of colleagues with whom the development of Intensive Interaction has been, and continues to be, a shared endeavour. They are too many to name but they will recognise the examples of their good practice within this book. Thanks are also due to Dorothy Foyle, Gemma Gray, John Harris, Mary Kellet, Judith Samuel and Lindsey Williams for their valuable feedback on the draft manuscript.

British Library Cataloguing in Publication Data

A CIP record for this book is available from the Public Library

ISBN 1 902519 63 9

© Copyright 2001 BILD Publications

BILD Publications is the publishing office of:
British Institute of Learning Disabilities
Wolverhampton Road
Kidderminster
Worcestershire
United Kingdom
DY10 3PP

Telephone: 01562 850251
Fax: 01562 851970
E-mail: bild@bild.demon.co.uk

Please contact BILD for a free publications catalogue listing BILD books, reports and training materials.

BILD Publications are distributed worldwide by
Plymbridge Distributors
Plymbridge House
Estover Road
Plymouth
United Kingdom
PL6 7PZ
Telephone: 01752 202301
Fax: 01752 202333

GLOSSARY

accountability being answerable to others and being responsible for our actions

age-appropriateness the idea of activities being appropriate for a person's chronological age; part of the normalisation ideal for people with learning disabilities

autistic spectrum disorders a term used to embrace autism, the autistic spectrum, Asperger's syndrome, and other pervasive developmental disorders

baseline the period before a new approach (intervention) is started

baseline assessment assessment of competence prior to the start of a new approach

behaviour modification a structured system of looking at behaviours and their triggers and pay-offs, in order to change someone's behaviour; behaviour modification manipulates the triggers and pay-offs (using rewards or negative consequences) to influence how often a behaviour recurs

behavioural approaches approaches based on behavioural psychology, that is, on the theory that people are best understood in terms of the way they behave and the factors that influence their behaviours (we repeat behaviour that results in positive consequences and don't repeat behaviour linked with negative consequences)

body language unspoken communication through body posture, gesture, even the way we dress or move our bodies; most body language is unconsciously delivered or interpreted

cause and effect the idea that 'when I do x, y happens', this involves the person with severe learning difficulties (SLD) understanding that they can have an effect on the world, the range of ways this can happen and the range of effects; social cause and effect involves understanding that we can cause another person to do (or feel) something

celebration in Intensive Interaction when we talk about celebrating the communicative behaviours of the person with SLD we don't mean having a party, but we do mean responding in a positive, hearty, perhaps lively and playful way, to show that the communications are noticed, welcomed and valued

communicative intent the intention to communicate; you need to be aware that you can communicate deliberately (i.e. influence another person's thoughts or feelings) to have communicative intent - this is more deliberate and active than reading another person's body language - see intentional communication

contingent responding responding that occurs soon after the behaviour responded to, and linked to it in some way; responding in a way that make these links immediate and obvious for a small child/person with disabilities (e g imitation)

delay procedures where the learner is encouraged to take their turn or play their role because there is a delay in teacher input and deliberately no verbal cue; the idea is to prevent dependence on prompts

developmental psychology the study of normal and abnormal development from infancy through the life stages

engagement a state of absorbed intellectual or emotional arousal and connectedness with another person (or an activity)

eye contact mutual looking, more specific than just looking at each other's faces; eye contact can be fleeting or lasting, warm or hostile etc, but it is a key part of communication and social interaction

Essential Lifestyle Planning a method of individual planning in adult services for people with learning difficulties which emphasises quality of listening to, and time spent with, the person

ethos the distinctive character or spirit or attitudes - the culture of a place or team

fundamentals of communication the early, basic, necessary foundations for all later communication to develop

generalisation general application of a new skill (or attitude or theory) to new situations or people

idiosyncratic communication a system of communication, understood by few, based on the particular behaviours or body language of an individual

imitation copying, doing what the other person does. In Intensive Interaction, imitating is a way of responding and connecting with the person with SLD, showing your willingness to get involved with them on their terms

incidental teaching an approach which involves arranging the natural environment so that it elicits initiations and communications

Intensive Interaction the specific interactive approach which forms the focus of this book; an approach to facilitating the development of social and communication abilities in people with SLD based on the model of caregiver-infant interaction

intentional communication communication that is intended rather than subconscious or accidental; becoming an intentional communicator, rather than someone for whom communications are ascribed, is an important development state - see communicative intent

interactive approaches a range of approaches in which the learner takes an active part in their learning, facilitated by the teacher's reciprocation, feedback and concern with the learning process rather than just the learning outcome

intrinsic motivation the motivation to do something because the thing itself is enjoyable or worth doing rather than for some unconnected reward or pay-off

intuition instinctive knowledge or insight, based on gut feeling rather than reason, not consciously thought out

joint attention two (or more) people attending to the same thing at the same time and aware of each other's attention; ability to jointly attend is necessary for conversation and other joint activity

motherese a term used to describe the talk style parents use with babies involving shorter sentences, simple vocabulary, varied pitch, lots of questions etc

movement therapy an approach, written about by Bronwyn Burford, in which reciprocal interactions are developed through imitating and joining in with the movement rhythms and patterns of the person with PMLD

mutual involvement a state of being involved with each other and aware of this, such as enjoying doing something together; through mutual involvement we learn about what each other is thinking and feeling and we develop shared meanings necessary for having conversations

objective assessment detached, unbiased assessment, not distorted by personal experience, feeling or knowledge

OFSTED Office for Standards in Education, the inspection board for schools

peer supervision a reciprocal system of supporting colleagues by listening and engaging in joint reflection, questioning and problem-solving

PMLD profound and multiple learning difficulties, that is, profound intellectual impairment combined with physical disability or sensory impairment

pre-verbal before speech has developed; the term also implies a stage before sign language or other symbolic communication

repertoire the range of interactive games that are familiar and within your experience; we need to build up a repertoire or catalogue of familiar games so that we can practise and explore without being bored or feeling threatened

room management a system for making best use of staff by clearly allocating different roles, including the role of overseeing, in order to free some staff up for concentrated work (e.g. quality one-to-one time)

safeguards (or safe practice guidelines) a set of rules or procedures designed to ensure the safety and respectful treatment of vulnerable people we work with, and to protect ourselves

self advocacy speaking up for yourself or making your own choices and decisions; the idea that people with learning disabilities should be in control of their own lives

self stimulation stimulating one's own senses, often in a stereotyped or ritualistic way; people with SLD may do this through rocking, grinding their teeth, poking fingers in their eyes etc; self stimulation may be pleasing because it is within the person's own control and safe and familiar for them

sensory/snoezelen rooms environments (with light shows, water-beds, sound -systems etc) created to stimulate the senses and bring this within the control of the child/person with disabilities through the use of adapted switches

signalling sending messages, often using body language or facial expression; Intensive Interaction involves becoming skilled at giving and reading non-verbal signals

subject assessment assessment that uses rather than denies previous knowledge and feelings; assessment based on involvement rather than detachment

symbolic communication a system of communication, understood by many, that uses some kind of symbol (word, sign, gesture, picture) to represent meaning

tuning-in the process of adapting to a person's signals (or language), of becoming familiar enough with them to be able to read them comfortably

turn-taking one of the fundamentals of communication, literally knowing you need to, and how to, take it in turns to vocalise or act

Waldon approach an approach advocated by Dr Geoffrey Waldon that involves children in repetitive manual activity with no verbal and little general interaction with adults

Chapter 1

INTRODUCTION

Sections in this chapter:

Why Intensive Interaction?

Who is Intensive Interaction for?

How do you 'do' Intensive Interaction?

How do babies learn to communicate and relate?

The principles of the parent interaction style with babies
Being available
Enjoyment
Let the baby lead
Responding
Creating and repeating familiar activities
Extending
Pausing

Applying the principles with people with SLD

Summary

WHY INTENSIVE INTERACTION?

This book is a practical guide to helping you to communicate more effectively with people with learning difficulties. It is also about helping you to help those people with learning difficulties you work with, or care for, to develop their communication abilities. We focus on communication because we believe it is the most important area to work on to make a difference to someone's quality of life.

We have organised the book in a way that we think will be user-friendly. In this chapter we begin with why you might want to use the approach and with whom. We also explain the principles and thinking behind the approach. Unless you have participated in training with us about Intensive Interaction, or read one of our other books, we urge you not to skip these sections because they are important to your understanding. They put the later practical chapters in context and enable you see how you might apply the principles in your own way. We then take you through the process of getting started with Intensive Interaction in Chapter Two and developing your abilities with the approach in Chapters Three and Four. Chapter Five gives guidance for moving on once you have achieved some success with the approach, or for when you are interacting with more able people with learning difficulties. In Chapter Six we look at the particular matters associated with using Intensive Interaction in the workplace. Wherever helpful we have given examples from our own experience or from the experience of colleagues practicing Intensive Interaction. We have included troubleshooting sections covering the types of challenges we have come across and summaries to help you to recap.

Human beings communicate with one another in complex ways that no other animals do, as far as we know. We have many languages using speech, but rich language communication is also possible with signing. There is more to communication than language, however. We also use eye contact, facial expressions, gestures, body language, physical contact. All these other aspects of communication often support the use of language, but people can communicate successfully simply by use of these other things. Consider how much emotional meaning may be given when one person simply places a hand on the shoulder of another. For many of us it is often an enjoyable thing simply to watch other people communicating. Indeed, it is a good exercise to watch people communicating and think about all of the different 'channels' of communication they are using.

Our communication abilities enable the human race to have society and culture, to build cities and roads, have television and music, to have organised governments, rules and systems and so on. The first purpose of human communication is something else however. We mostly communicate with one another because communication itself is enjoyable, interesting, fulfiling, emotionally rewarding, it enables us to be close to other people, to have relationships. Think about how many of your communications during the course of the day have no outcome or product. Much of what we communicate with one another is the sort of 'hot air' of companionship. We often talk to each other about trivial things, frequently generating fun and laughter. This ability to relate with each other simply for the purpose of relating seems to be central to being contented, to our emotional well-being. Mostly, most of us simply like to be with other people and enjoy each other, talk, laugh, be companions.

> "Hi, how are you doing"?
>
> "I'm okay, the weather is really getting me down though."
>
> "Yeah, I hate it when the nights draw in like this."
>
> "Three months of dark mornings and greyness all day."
>
> "Yeah, I should have been born a squirrel - I could ignore it all and go to sleep."
>
> "Ha, ha, I wouldn't like all the nuts."

The people we are concerned with in this book usually don't have the same rich and complex communication abilities that most of the rest of us share easily. Their learning difficulties have included not achieving full use of language. Actually, most of the people we are thinking about will have very limited understanding of language. Many of them are people who seem to have very few general communication abilities and some may have a lifestyle where they seem lonely and remote, relating only briefly with the people around them.

This is why Intensive Interaction has been developed. Intensive Interaction is a practical approach to working with people with very severe learning difficulties and just spending time with them, which helps them to relate and communicate better with the people around them. It is a good way of going about this because it is based on how communication ordinarily develops - on ways we know are effective - and in ways we know can be enjoyable for all involved.

WHO IS INTENSIVE INTERACTION FOR?

The people the approach is aimed at do not form one group that we can describe easily. There are various terms associated with the people who Intensive Interaction is intended for: people who are pre-verbal, or pre-lingual (that is, without speech); people who are difficult to reach (that is, seeming to prefer to be away from human contact); people with profound and multiple learning difficulties, people with severe and complex learning difficulties; people with 'autistic spectrum disorders', particularly those with developmental delay. What these people have in common is poorly developed social and communication abilities, usually accompanied by additional learning, sensory or behavioural difficulties.

Intensive Interaction is also for people of all ages. It is clearly beneficial that the approach is used as early as possible in the lives of children with severe learning difficulties and in partnership with the parents or carers, since they, in the home situation, are potentially the best teachers of these abilities. However, adults too can benefit from improved communication abilities at any stage of their lives.

Bharti, aged 17

Bharti used to sit in her wheelchair, seeming not very interested in people or the world, sleeping often. She did sometimes make little noises and staff got into the habit of making sure they enjoyably imitated these noises. Over nine months or so, she progressed to making a great deal of noise, laughing and shrieking, attracting the attention of staff and demanding communication. Her use of eye contact and facial expressions became captivating too, and staff found little difficulty enjoying giving her attention.

Lee, aged 12

Lee was a boy who wouldn't, couldn't sit down. In fact he spent most of his day in frenetic activity, wandering or running or skipping around the classroom, frequently climbing on furniture and windowsills, sweeping equipment off table-tops and barging into other people's activities. He could not speak, but seemed to understand language, though he seemed to choose not to attend to other people, preferring his own wild activity, laughing frequently, seeming sometimes to be almost hysterical.

At first, as a survival tactic, Carol started taking him out of the classroom to the soft-play room or the quiet side-room. In those situations, she found that it was much easier to tolerate and even enjoy his behaviour. She experimented with joining-in, moving with Lee, joining-in with his laughter. Lee clearly enjoyed this and started to take hold of Carol. She found that they frequently ended up in face-to-face situations, with moments of Lee giving her sparkling attention. Carol realised that these were good moments, and she started looking for them.

After a few weeks, she found that she could even engineer these 'still times' and she began to work at extending them and having them happen more frequently. Soon, she was able to have some good quiet moments with Lee during circle-time, in the classroom.

John, aged 26

When staff started using Intensive Interaction with John, he was a person who spent virtually all his time wandering alone, involved in a variety of rhythmic activities. During two years he progressed to being able to take part in interaction sessions for more than five minutes, clearly enjoying the mutual experience with another person. He learnt to use a range of qualities of eye contact, developed an increasing range of facial expressions, to take turns in a variety of ways in activities within interactions. His lifestyle gradually changed and he was less self-absorbed, often seeking a person rather than his own rhythmic activity.

Camilla, aged 45

Camilla has a diagnosis of autism. She spends her time mostly silent and alone, usually rocking and pulling at her lip. Staff worked patiently to help her enjoy being with them by sensitive use of Intensive Interaction principles. Camilla could only put up with a little company, so staff left her as soon as she looked uncomfortable.

Gradually she started to turn toward them, then smile, then to laugh as something silly happened.

Hayley, aged 4

Hayley is a little girl who potentially did not have learning difficulties. She had been brought up in difficult family circumstances and completely neglected. At first, staff in the respite home found her to be wild and unpredictable. They went back to basics and started to use Intensive Interaction to teach Hayley the earliest abilities. Gradually, but then quite quickly, the activities developed and developed. Two years later, Hayley seemed to have language virtually appropriate to her age, though she was still a little wild.

In order to make this book easier to use we will simplify some of the language we use to talk about the people involved with Intensive Interaction. We will use 'people with SLD' to generally refer to any of the people in the descriptions above. We will also use 'communication partner' to refer to the staff member, professional, carer or family member involved in Intensive Interaction with them.

Below we give some examples of what we might call **the fundamentals of communication** - the basic, necessary foundations for all communication to develop. Most of us use these abilities in various combinations without thinking about them much. When we are with other people, we are using these skills simultaneously, second by second. The ability to do this complicated operation is a wonderful human thing. Surprisingly perhaps, the learning of these complicated abilities starts at birth. In fact, babies have to learn a great deal about these fundamentals during their first year. It is necessary for them to know about them before they can learn speech. If babies do not learn these things, it is much less likely that they will learn speech and language. These items in the box are the foundations of communication and language, indeed the building blocks of everything else that a person goes on to learn. If a developing person does not learn these fundamental things, it will not only make learning language much less likely, but it will make it more difficult to learn anything else. It will also make it more difficult to make sense of the world and to have an impact on it.

Some Fundamentals of Communication
- use and understanding of eye contact

- use of facial expressions

- learning to 'read' facial expressions

- learning to enjoy giving attention to another person

- taking turns in exchanges of behaviour

- use and understanding of physical contact

- use and understanding of gestures

- learning to 'read' body language

- learning about personal space

- learning to concentrate and attend

So, with Intensive Interaction we are trying to help people with SLD to learn some of these important abilities. The emphasis really is on the practical. The idea is for the communication partner to create enjoyable social situations with the other person - brief one-to-one interaction sessions. The content of the interaction is simply what takes place between the two people using face, voice and body language. These sessions will provide opportunities for the person with SLD to rehearse using and understanding the fundamentals of communication. The sessions also provide opportunities for the communication partners to get to know them, like them and build a relationship with them.

Other things will probably happen too:

- challenging behaviours may generally improve and the person may become easier to be with

- the person may simply become happier, seeming to enjoy life better

- it may be much easier to get their attention in order to do anything

- it may be possible to involve the person in more and more new activities

- the person may become more assertive generally, seeking out attention and other people's company, even when this is inconvenient!

- a person who was always remote may start to be more comfortable as a member of a group

- basic care activities such as washing and dressing may become easier, with the person taking greater interest and participating more

Each person we work with will make different types of progress. For the person who has a lifestyle of being alone in a corner, concentrating on repetitive behaviour, getting that person to come away from the corner and enjoy and take interest in other people for a few minutes may be a major lifestyle achievement. More may then be possible, but just that will have a major positive effect on that individual's life.

Some people may make consistent, on-going progress, taking part in, and perhaps demanding, many social experiences each day. They can become increasingly interested in and confident about everything around them. Their lives may therefore flourish and open up, with all sorts of new experiences becoming possible. Some people do progress to more and more communication with voice, developing a range of meaningful noises, some may even progress to some use of speech.

HOW DO YOU 'DO' INTENSIVE INTERACTION?

Hopefully it will be clear by now that the major resource for Intensive Interaction activities is you - the communication partner. The main idea is for you to:

1. Relax and enjoy yourself with the person with SLD and allow some of your natural communication abilities to guide what you do.

2. At the same time, think carefully about how to have a successful interaction with this person, by using some simple principles borrowed from the interaction style parents use with infants.

Throughout the book, we will be offering guidance on these principles and how the approach is carried out, but it is important to remember that it is **you**, your face, voice and body language, your personality which makes the material for the activities. It is possible to find members of staff in all services who seem to be very good, 'naturals' without ever having heard of Intensive Interaction. They have simply used their natural abilities and human understandings to work out how to communicate and relate with people who do not find this at all easy. More usually though, people learn this through the help of others, staff training and reading and using guidance like this book.

Staff working together at SLD schools in long stay hospitals in Hertfordshire developed Intensive Interaction as an approach, both by using their natural abilities (their intuitions), and by looking carefully at what is known about how babies learn to communicate and be social. Most of the principles of Intensive Interaction are based on this normal pattern of development and so you will see frequent reference to them in this book. Intensive Interaction is also about trial and error, preferably within supportive teams, and you will still need to experiment to find what works for you. The next section briefly describes how adults help babies to become communicators. This is explained further in the following chapters.

HOW DO BABIES LEARN TO COMMUNICATE AND RELATE?

Babies learn a huge amount in their first year. As mentioned, the learning is very complicated. What the adults do in order to help the baby learn these things is also very skilled and complex. Yet strangely, when the conditions are right, this all comes together in a way that seems very straightforward.

As we all must be aware the moment we start thinking about it, the best learning for a baby about how to be a communicator happens in situations where they are with another person. Babies tend to get frequent interactions with adults throughout the day, for all sorts of reasons. There is all the caring to be done - washing, changing, feeding, bathing, dressing and undressing, putting to bed. However, most parents and most other available adults, also like to have 'conversations' with babies - interactions where they are just with them for the pleasure of being with them. These interactions are usually light-hearted, full of fun, with the

Age-appropriateness?

We are basing the communication style of the communication partner on how babies learn complicated things successfully with adults. There may seem to be apparent conflict with important ideas of age-appropriateness in our work. We suggest that there is not conflict. It is now common in our services to observe staff who do everything they can to give proper importance to the age and adult status of a person with SLD. At the same time, the staff recognise the reality that this is a person who is at an early stage of development. To be happy and fulfilled, this person may also need communication experiences which are full of fun, relaxed and understandable to that person. Doing both of these things is important. See Chapter 4 for more discussion of this issue.

adult face-to-face with the baby, exchanging eye contact and facial expression, talking and making noises, especially making the noises the baby makes. The main intention seems to be to enjoy spending time together. Of course, many of the care situations, bathing and so on, tend to involve these warm interactive games too.

Throughout the first year, these interactions become longer and longer, with more and more things happening in them. They become more and more like conversations and during the second year, they begin to involve the baby starting to use speech as well. By that time though, the baby is very good at giving attention and concentrating for many minutes, taking turns, watching for signals and reading the other person's signals, watching and reading the adult's face for meanings, making a huge range of communicative noises. This development of the ability to communicate and have interactions continues throughout childhood and on into adulthood.

During the first year particularly, adults have a particular style of behaviour which enables the baby to take part in these interactions successfully. This style also helps the baby to learn how to be a communicator. This style is very natural - when we are doing it we are not thinking much about what it is we do. It is more difficult to have this natural style, that psychologists have shown to be helpful for development, when the baby has a disability or learning difficulty. The style is usually maintained by the baby's positive response to it - by smiles and eye contact and cooing. If the baby is unresponsive, or slow to respond, or responding in a way that is not typical, it is easy for the adult to become stressed. We are likely to alter our interaction style by working harder and making demands on the baby to 'look at me' and so on.

However, it is possible to analyse what takes place, in the most relaxed of interactions, the kind we know have a positive effect on development, even in babies with disabilities. It is possible to identify the special things that the adult does, and from this to describe some rough 'rules' or principles for the way that the adult style works. In Intensive Interaction we use these principles, while all the time recognising that the person with SLD may not be a baby or even a child. The role for you, the communication partner, is to know about and use these principles creatively during the Intensive Interaction sessions. They can provide a framework for how you should behave, but the main thing is for you to relax and be creative in your use of these principles. There is no 'one way' to 'do' Intensive Interaction.

WE DO NOT

- dominate and direct

- try to get the baby to do the Times crossword with us

- talk about last night's soaps

- talk in full, complete, adult sentences

- give orders, make demands

- set an objective for the conversation and write a plan

- basically, we do not do adult things at an adult level, expecting the baby to be interested

WE DO

- make ourselves available to have a conversation at the baby's level of understanding

- watch the baby carefully for any sign of interest and enjoyment

- respond to things the baby doe, let the baby lead

- celebrate facial expressions and noises - often by imitating or joining in

- keep the conversation going by enjoying what the baby does and:

- by taking pauses, go at the baby's pace

THE PRINCIPLES OF THE PARENT INTERACTION STYLE WITH BABIES

BEING AVAILABLE

It is not possible for adults simply to demand that a three-month-old baby gives them attention. We accept that a young baby may have limited abilities to do that and that if we are to get attention and have a conversation, we have to win that attention. So, the adult style is about capturing the interest and attention of someone with limited abilities. We have to make sure that everything we do in a conversation with a three-month-old is interesting and enjoyable to that person. The way that we go about doing this is by making sure that everything that takes place during the conversation is understandable for a three-month-old.

One of the key things we do is to make ourselves available to that person in order to have a conversation with them on their terms.

We make ourselves available to a baby frequently. We give them plenty of time and attention. There are some important things happening as we make ourselves available. We get our face in the right place. For a very young baby, the most important thing for them to see is an adult face, so we are careful to be in a position where our faces are easily available so that the baby can see it without effort. There is a feeling that we are joining the baby in their world, by making ourselves available on their terms. Everything that happens must feel secure, comfortable and understandable. Babies are easily upset and distracted, so we also make ourselves available by not rushing anything and by making the experience as relaxed and enjoyable as possible.

ENJOYMENT

Enjoyment is one of the basic principles of the adult style. For an interaction between an adult and a baby to be truly successful and feel mutual, both people need to enjoy themselves. This mutual enjoyment helps the baby to feel relaxed and secure. It also enables the content of the activity to be interesting and motivating for the baby. It means, too, that all of the learning that the baby does in these situations is of course, relaxed and enjoyable. It will also mean that both baby and adult will want to come back for more!

LET THE BABY LEAD

Surprising as it might seem, during these interactions it is the baby who mostly leads the activity. The way in which adults make themselves available to the baby has already been described above. It goes further than that. We could say that the adults make themselves available to be enjoyably used by the baby as a plaything. The baby finds the adult interesting in all sorts of ways, but the main thing is that the baby can creatively use the adult as a sort of 'activity centre'. The baby can try out all sorts of behaviours with an adult and see if they work. Adults do one fundamentally important thing in order to let the baby lead - adults **respond** to things that the baby does.

RESPONDING

Basically, babies learn to communicate very quickly, because in interactions with adults, the adults create conversations by responding to things that the baby does. For the baby, this makes the content easy to understand and enjoy. The adult being responsive is another of the important principles of the interaction style that is effective with babies, perhaps the most important or central principle. It helps the baby keep on learning new and different ways of behaving in interactions with adults. The baby tries out new noises or movements or facial expressions, and the adult responds, often by doing it again, imitating or joining in. We can call these responses the adult celebrations of what the baby did. Naturally, these **celebrations** are very pleasing and rewarding for the baby, making it more likely that the baby will do the same thing again.

CREATING AND REPEATING FAMILIAR ACTIVITIES

These interactions happen many times during the first few months. The parents and the baby build up shared knowledge of things that they can do together. They create a sort of catalogue or **repertoire** of these activities which they repeat many times in order to enjoy each other frequently and to have what feels like a conversation. Therefore, day-by-day, the baby is learning about a wide range of things they can do which are effective in getting enjoyable responses from the parents. Of course, the parents don't really think about it like this, they are just behaving naturally, being relaxed, having fun and being playful. They laugh and smile, make noises when the baby does, speak in short sentences with a melodic voice. Having these experiences enables the baby to learn and rehearse crucial skills like attending, exploring and interpreting facial expressions.

Turn-taking

Being able to take turns with the other person is a crucial skill for all of us when we are having interactions. We started learning how to do it more or less from the word go.

Babies learn turn-taking by making noises, by doing things with their faces, and with movements. Adults insert bits of their own behaviour, often imitations of the baby, in between the bursts of the baby's behaviour. This creates turns without the baby realising it at first. Soon, however, the pleasure of exchanging bursts of behaviour, and real turn-taking emerges. As the first year progresses, turn-taking activities become more complicated involving toys and objects and increasingly speech-like vocalisations.

EXTENDING

While parents and babies are repeating these familiar interaction routines, new things happen as well. The baby might deliberately or intentionally experiment - try out new things to see what happens. If the adults see this and respond then this new interaction will probably also be added to the repertoire.

The adults will also be doing something more. When something is working well in an interaction for both the parents and the baby, the parents are likely to try and keep that moment going. They will try to extend it, make it last a little longer. The parents may make yet more repetitions, sometimes with a little mock drama in their faces and voices, sometimes with a sense of playful tease. While they are doing this, they are also getting the baby to make further responses to things that they do. The creation of **turn-taking** is an important aspect of the development of the interactions in the first year.

PAUSING

An important aspect of the parent's responsive style is that they allow pauses during the interactions. During the activities, there will be many moments when perhaps not much is happening, or the baby simply goes quiet, takes a rest. If the parents are being effectively responsive, then they will respond by taking a pause themselves. In fact we know that it is crucial that adults use pauses in this way. Driving on, urging or demanding that the baby keep going doesn't work, it is likely to have the opposite effect. Babies participate most effectively when everything is relaxed and they are more or less leading the activity and controlling the pace. We can go so far as to say that the pauses are a vital part of being responsive and part of the interaction.

By the end of the first year, if everything has been working well, a baby has considerable abilities to communicate and do all sorts of things. The activities between the parents and their baby will have continued developing in a sort of 'snowball' effect. The baby will be set up further learning with good foundations for further development and feeling good about themselves and others.

Further Reading

If you would like to look at some of the literature on parent-infant interaction directly yourself, we recommend any of the following:

Schaffer's old but classic *Studies in Mother-Infant Interaction* (1977, Academic Press) or new (1996) *Social Development* (Routledge); Bullowa's (1979) *Before Speech* (Cambridge University Press); Lewis & Rosenblum's (1974) *The Effect of the Infant on its Caregiver* (Wiley).

APPLYING THE PRINCIPLES WITH PEOPLE WITH SLD

It is these good foundations for further learning and good self-esteem that we need to work on with people with SLD. Without the principles above we might not know where to start on enabling these to develop. All kinds of approaches have been used with people with SLD for all kinds of purposes. We know we can use very structured behaviourist programmes to teach skills like dressing or to stop behaviours like spitting. We know we can provide materials like sand and paint and clay to encourage development of hand skills and thinking and creativity. We know we can stimulate people with PMLD with music and smell and lights. We do not know, however, other ways to give people solid foundations for further learning, or to give them the motivation and basic abilities to be social and communicative. It is for this reason that the principles of the interactive style parents use with babies is directly relevant for us in our work and care for people with SLD.

In the remainder of this book we will illustrate how the principles can be applied. At no time do we advocate treating people with SLD who are not babies as if they were babies. We show how the way of interacting can be a respectful and meaningful way of interacting with older people with SLD. We show how using the principles leads to all sorts of other good practice. Using the style is inevitably different when the person we are interacting with has SLD and we discuss the issues that arise from this. We also give practical guidance on what this might mean for what we do and how we do it. You will notice that some aspects of the style fit very well with ideas about self-advocacy and making your own choices. You will also be aware of all the additional layers of thinking and reflecting and problem-solving and teamwork that are involved in applying the style in more challenging circumstances.

We have found the style incredibly useful for guiding the way we are generally with people with SLD, and for providing a focus for quality one-to-one work with our students. The challenge in this practical guide is to make Intensive Interaction accessible to busy people without over-simplifying the more complex and subtle aspects of the approach. We list below some of the key principles of the interactive style, but urge that these be used as a reminder of this chapter and not just as checklist.

- being available

- being observant and tuned in

- being responsive

- relaxing and enjoying the interaction

- being warm and playful

- celebrating responses and new behaviours

- allowing pauses

- letting the baby/person with SLD lead

- creating and repeating familiar mutually enjoyable interactions

- extending your responses to become turn-taking and other new developments

SUMMARY

- Intensive Interaction is an approach to helping people with very severe learning difficulties to learn more about communicating and relating.

- By using Intensive Interaction we are trying to help the person learn fundamentals of communication - eye contacts, facial expressions, turn-taking etc.

- The people we work with will develop in various ways. For some, even a little progress in communicating may have a major lifestyle effect.

- In doing Intensive Interaction activities the member of staff attempts to create enjoyable and understandable interactions with the other person.

- The member of staff is the major resource for the approach.

- In their first year, babies are involved in frequent pleasurable interactions with adults.

- A crucial aspect of the adult style is to build these activities by responding to things the baby does.

- By doing this the adults and the baby create a repertoire of familiar activities which they repeat frequently.

- These activities extend and grow, and by being involved in them, the baby establishes good foundations for later learning and good self-esteem.

- The principles of parent-baby interaction provide the guiding framework for how to interact with people with SLD in Intensive Interaction.

Chapter 2

GETTING STARTED

Sections in this chapter:

Deciding who you will use the approach with

What will it be like to work with Intensive Interaction?

Preparation
> *Don't be in a rush*
> *Give yourself time to observe*
> *Allow yourself to absorb*
> *Do you already interact?*
> *Do a baseline*
> *Finding quality time*
> *Team preparation*

Summary

DECIDING WHO YOU WILL USE THE APPROACH WITH

You may be a classroom assistant or teacher in an SLD school, or a nursery, a day service worker, or a member of home support staff, or someone who is interested in becoming a befriender or advocate for a person with SLD. You the reader, may well be a carer or parent of a child or adult with SLD, who feels that there is yet more progress to be made, at home even, with your child's ability to communicate and relate. Probably what you all have in common is that you know or work with at least one person with SLD who has limited ability to make contact with the people around them, and what you want for them is that they could do more. Some of you will be working with groups of people with SLD and you may feel a little overwhelmed by how many people you have who need this approach. How do you select among them, or do you just try and get going with all of them all at once?

If you have not tried the approach before it is a good idea to go very easy on yourself. Start slowly, carefully think about and organise what you are doing and don't overwhelm yourself with experiences. Give yourself time to gain experience gradually before taking on too much all at once.

We would advise starting off and trying things out with just one person. This could be the person with whom you judge you have the best chance of being successful. (You may be better equipped to help more challenging people having got some experience of success with one person.) This might involve working with someone who clearly already has some knowledge and ability with the fundamentals of communication. This may be someone with whom you have already established some kind of relationship. It may be someone you feel can do some communicative things and already has a degree of comfort in social situations and is approachable. Perhaps it is a person who already approaches you and attempts to interact, but you are often at a loss to know how to respond in a way which keeps the experience going for both of you.

Alternatively, you could try first with the person who seems in most extreme need. This is more likely to be someone who is difficult for you and others to be with. You need good teamwork for this (see Chapter Six) as it may not be easy. However, the feeling of effectiveness you gain from small breakthroughs here is likely to sustain you through future work, and the change in quality of life for the person with SLD may be very significant.

WHAT WILL IT BE LIKE TO WORK WITH INTENSIVE INTERACTION?

For many staff or parents doing Intensive Interaction does not involve a radical change of interactive style or a very new way of doing things. It is more an endorsement of how they want to be with people with SLD and 'permission' to spend more time and thought on it. For others though, it will be quite new. More than anything else, when you embark on Intensive Interaction you should be looking forward to having **fun**. You should become a practitioner of the approach who is relaxed and at ease with what you are trying to do. The work itself, creating the sessions, means that you will be 'playful', **lighthearted, responsive** and **flexible**. It may mean working in a variety of different places. You should be prepared for instance, to be on the floor if that is the preferred place of the person with SLD you are trying to help.

You may also find that some sessions can become physically active and involve moving around the room, even becoming something of a physical romp. Many people with SLD as they start learning to relate, do what most people who are at an early stage of development do - they use a lot of **physical contact**. The judgement as to whether you are going to give physical contact in return should be an individual one based on your assessment of that person's needs. It needs to be borne in mind that touch is a very basic form of communication and that understanding about touch can only be gained from experiencing it.

So on the one hand you may need to be or become a member of staff who is fairly comfortable with exuberant behaviour, perhaps comfortable with touching and being touched. On the other hand, not all Intensive

---

Physical Contact

Physical contact is a very important form of communication for babies. It is also important in that it gives reassurance and security. It is a very basic form of communication which can make quite complicated messages easily understood.

It is inevitable that many people with SLD, of whatever age, may need to receive physical contact and indeed may demand it. There can be a tendency in work place situations to refuse physical contact on the grounds that it is 'not appropriate'.

We need to bear in mind the very important purpose of physical contact for a person who is at an early stage of development. Issues of 'appropriateness' may not be as important to that person as an understandable human need.

We, the authors of this book are not in favour of having rules which deny people physical contact. We are in favour of judging each person's needs individually and differently. Sometimes that means gladly giving physical contact and appreciating the importance of it for the other person. It may also mean dealing with potential difficulties which may arise for the person with SLD or for staff. It implies staff working together talking and having good, supportive teamwork.

Interaction sessions are lively and physical. Many of them are quiet and gentle - some people, you may find, like all of their sessions to be quiet and gentle.

For staff, there is no particular personality type which is more suited to doing Intensive Interaction. It is tempting to think that extroverts are going to be the most effective communication partners. However, extroverts can sometimes crowd an interaction with too much behaviour. In the introduction, it was stressed that part of the skill for you, the communication partner, is to avoid 'flooding' the interaction session with your own behaviour. Especially in the early stages, most of your behaviour needs to be held back so that you can make time and space available for the other person to produce behaviour to which you then respond. Your response may well be exuberant, full of fun, but carefully timed to reward the person with SLD for doing something communicative.

Intuition?

A teacher who was very good and experienced at doing Intensive Interaction was asked how she did it. To what extent was she deciding what to do, moment by moment by thinking about 'rules' or principles? To what extent was she simply relaxing, letting her natural ability as a communicator guide her? She responded:

" I don't know really. I suppose if I think about it I'm more or less on autopilot most of the time when I'm interacting. I suppose most of the time I'm responding and doing things pretty intuitively, without thinking about it much. Maybe twenty per cent of the time I have to think about oh right, what shall I do next. That's when I will think about you know, principles that can guide me.

I suppose when I started a few years ago I was thinking consciously a bit more. These days I guess I've done plenty and learnt to let it flow naturally."

Over time you will become even more sensitive as a communicator than you are now. You will learn to appreciate consciously the tiny things that people can do which are a communication. You will become a person who can 'tune-in' to other individuals easily. Your performance as an interaction partner will be about finding your own happy blend of letting your natural abilities lead you, together with the need to think sometimes in a conscious, technical way about things like: "now, what shall I do next?". Of course, you can meet people who are so natural at doing the approach that they never seem to need to think about it. In fact, it is hoped that many of you reading this book will be experiencing the thought - "oh I already do quite a lot of this naturally, it seems like the right thing to do to get x smiling and interested."

Many members of staff who adopt the approach mention other things that happen to them over a period of time. There can be a natural process of gradually doing everything during the day in a more relaxed, more fun way. One person reported being less forceful, using less physical prompting in order to organise his group. He discovered he didn't need to be so directive since he was communicating better and was more effective in getting people's attention. A member of staff in a residential establishment talked about how she now made activities more lively and light-hearted. It was much easier to get her residents to participate in doing something like the washing-up. A member of staff in working in secure accommodation claimed the approach had made him a better defuser of challenging situations - 'reading' signs and signals much better, appreciating how people were feeling at an earlier stage.

Overall, working with Intensive Interaction should help you to appreciate the balance between 'being' and 'doing'. Intensive Interaction enables you to be with people with SLD in a highly constructive and purposeful way, but without making demands, or giving them another task to do, and without expecting to reach a visible outcome to the activity.

PREPARATION

DON'T BE IN A RUSH

The most important thing to remember in your preparation is don't be in a rush. First and foremost, it is not the kind of work that you can do in a rush. In fact, stress and urgency will not help at all. The watchwords for starting out with the approach are: **relax, respond** and **enjoy**. In fact, let's go further. The best way to carry out the approach is to be very kind to yourself. You are very valuable, you are an instrument, a resource, you are the material which makes the communication partner. What takes place is going to take place because you use yourself well. You will only truly be available as a communication partner if you are in good shape, fairly relaxed, prepared to enjoy yourself.

GIVE YOURSELF TIME TO OBSERVE

First of all, think about who it is you are going to start working with, bearing in mind the advice at the start of this chapter. The next thing is to try and organise it so that you have a little time, each day if possible, to do some observations. This need not be a great deal of time, but it is valuable time. Of course, to organise this you may need to get the co-operation of colleagues and it may seem a difficult thing to do. It is worth remembering that your team needs to organise so that you and others can be free for periods of the day to do focused one-to-one work (see Chapter Six). So, organising these observations is good rehearsal.

ALLOW YOURSELF TO ABSORB

You may have known the person you are going to be interacting with for a long time. Nevertheless, it is still worth trying to do some observation and without being too objective in the way you observe. In fact, we recommend doing the opposite. By being very subjective you allow yourself to really get to know something more about that person's behaviour and lifestyle. Allow yourself some time to look and absorb. Remember too, that observing in this way means being relaxed. We are not talking about the sort of observation where you sit in the corner with a clipboard. Get yourself comfortable somewhere, maybe sitting or lying and just take in the world.

These observations may well tell you all sorts of new things. In our busy working day we can be so stressed-up about needing to get things done that we can miss something very obvious - we can actually fail to give people good quality attention in the way that they want it or need it. Plus, there is the issue that what we are trying to do here is something very basic and **normal** and **human**. We are going to try and communicate with another person in a way that they can understand. That is all. There is always the danger that we can get overly technical and objective and lose the sense of the person somewhere along the way.

There is also a sensitive issue which needs sensitive attention. The person you are attempting to work with may not only be a person who finds it difficult to be with other people, but also a person who is very difficult to be with. They may have frequent outbursts of challenging behaviour. They may have unattractive or unappealing habits which discourage others from being near them. Part of the process of observation at this time may be about discovering, perhaps for the first time, a range of positive things about the person, especially behaviours which do not repel. These behaviours you have observed may form the first focus for your attempts at responding.

DO YOU ALREADY INTERACT?

Let's say you are intending to interact with Annette and she isn't yet able to give good attention to another person. As part of the preparation, you may also like to think carefully and maybe make some notes about whether you have already been finding little moments with her, moments where you have succeeded in 'lighting her up' a little. By 'lighting her up', we mean moments where you do something with your behaviour which just catches her attention properly. The result may be a swivelled glance, a change in posture, a clap of the hands, a smile or even laughter and eye contact.

Probably you have always thought about those moments as "just mucking about". However, consider their importance in the light of what you have read so far here. Those were moments when you cleverly used your behaviour to get true attention from a person who has a great deal of difficulty in giving it. Not only that, for Annette it was a moment of real mutual togetherness and enjoyment with another person. Try to remember how those moments were created and how you used yourself. You might even have established a routine of 'mucking about' with Annette. In this case you and Annette already have a little repertoire of interactive activities - actually, you have already started with an interactive approach.

DO A BASELINE

However, just to be technical and stand back for a minute, at this stage it may really be worth your while worth doing some documentation. The idea is to record Annette's starting point. To put it another way, in a year's time, for Annette's sake, and for yours, you need to be sure how far you have come from the start point and know just how much Annette has learnt. The assessment documentation you do at this stage is often known as a baseline. It shouldn't involve a great deal of work and it isn't too technical, merely a matter of making sure that you write down everything that you know about Annette's present communication abilities. If you are familiar with using video, this can be a very useful way of making some recording also. Further advice is given on record-keeping in Chapter Six.

FINDING QUALITY TIME

An important aspect of preparation at this stage is to start thinking about how you, and probably your colleagues, will be organising yourselves in order to carry out Intensive Interaction sessions with Annette. The first thing to be considered is that you will need to find some quality one-to-one time. In most places where we work with people with SLD, there is usually an ethic that staff organise themselves in order to make sure that people get one-to-one time. However, there can also be an increasing tendency, in schools for instance, to do groupwork, particularly for National Curriculum subject teaching. People who are at early levels of development learn best in focused one-to-one situations. They usually have difficulty being a member of a group or may be a passive member of that group, not being able to give good attention to the group task. It is vital that their quality time for communication activities is organised.

Getting one-to-one time

If you or your team are having difficulty organising one-to-one time, it is a good idea to remember one thing. Intensive Interaction sessions are mostly brief, especially in the early stages. Brief could mean just a few seconds a few times a day. By the time the interaction session takes a minute or more of sustained attention from both people, things are going really well. Five minutes or more is a very long session and it is likely that the person with SLD is a very active participant, taking part in extended turn-taking.

- Perhaps the staff group you are working in already has systems for organising one-to-one time for each person.

- If you haven't, perhaps you and your colleagues should consider it and talk about it. Receiving good quality one-to- one attention is important for all people with SLD, but essential for people who are pre-verbal.

There are many potential barriers to providing good quality time, it is a good idea to look at them and what can be done to overcome them.

- Perhaps some discussion is necessary with your manager. It may help to change some systems or working structures a little. It may be the case that in your workplace, there is a heavy emphasis on involving people with SLD in productive-looking activities which have a visible outcome every time. Intensive Interaction activities will not be like this. Your staff group and perhaps your manager may need to discuss the way in which these fun-filled interactions are actually serious work.

- You may be working in a school, probably with at least two members of staff in a class team. It should be possible to use a room management system for part of the day. This means organising so that one person does group activities or 'holds the fort', while the other moves from person-to-person. This is a commonly-seen approach.

- Equally, this should be possible in day centres for adults, though the staffing can be less than in a school and the groups bigger.

- In residential work, it should be possible to find an incidental few minutes every day, in an already relaxed and informal setting.

- Don't forget, all basic care activities are good one-to-one time. Don't rush through them. Make them an enjoyable, quality experience for the person with SLD. They are good opportunities for communication.

- If you are a parent of a child with SLD you might like to think about how some of these suggestions for staff might help, particularly having play whilst doing care and organising for just a few minutes of relaxed, taskless play where you do nothing but enjoy your child.

TEAM PREPARATION

If you and your colleagues are not previously accustomed to working in this way, then some general team preparation will be advisable. Team issues are dealt with at more length in Chapter Six. However, what needs to take place at this preparation stage, is in a general sense not especially difficult or complicated, but team issues can get in the way of doing Intensive Interaction work. The list below gives a range of points to consider and probably discuss. Intensive Interaction is an approach which really needs good teamwork and people with SLD will benefit most if they have several members of staff (or family) who are all available as potential communication partners. The approach will work best if these team members are well prepared, if they are working together with shared understandings and appreciate what they are attempting to do and why. The achievement of shared understandings and a shared value system is often the most difficult area of teamwork. A team can find itself in the situation that individuals work or interact with the same person in different ways because each of those members of staff look at life differently. There are advantages to this for the person with SLD. However, when it comes to managing challenging behaviours, communication issues or emotional support, then it is likely that differences between staff will negatively affect the life of the person you are attempting to help.

Team Preparation Issues

- There needs to be discussion of practical organisation to promote quality one-to-one time if these systems are not already in place.

- You should discuss with colleagues and preferably management, what the approach will be like.

- Ideally, the team will arrive at the shared value that the development of communication is the most important single issue for a person with SLD

- Stress to your colleagues that Intensive Interaction is a relaxed and informal thing to do, that you would like them to join in, but perhaps when they feel comfortable to do so.

- Stress also that the interaction sessions do not have an immediately visible outcome. The outcomes can be seen gradually over a period of time.

- As previously suggested, do good record-keeping. It may be necessary to demonstrate success to your colleagues.

- You may need to have discussion particularly about staff and management attitudes with regard to normalisation, age-appropriateness and physical contact.

Tanya is having a supervision with Claude, the boss.

"So Tanya, you want to do this Intensive Interaction thing with Annette?"

"Yes"

"And will it involve a lot of laughter and enjoying yourselves?"

"Yes"

"Tanya, life isn't just about enjoying yourself you know. We need to do some serious work with Annette."

"Claude, what I want to do with Annette is serious and it is work!"

It is, of course, not the best situation if you have colleagues who do not understand, who perhaps giggle or criticise when you do an Intensive Interaction session. Naturally, it is good teamwork on your part to attempt to help them understand, by showing them this book for instance, or being determined to keep talking to them. In such a situation some members of staff have simply had to press on alone for a while, and then, at a later stage, change the attitudes of their colleagues by showing good results in the communication development of the person they are working with.

There are many stories about getting started with this approach. Part of the difficulty is that the way of working can seem to be so different from other ways of working. Yet it is always so important to stress that what is being undertaken is natural, relaxed, failure-free.

Avril

Avril is a day-centre social worker in the 'Special Needs' group of a Social Education Centre. She wanted to use Intensive Interaction with Kevin, a young man with autism in her group. None of her colleagues was interested in helping. Indeed they were dismissive of her wishes and they made fun of her. Avril went ahead on her own. Kevin turned out to be very responsive, benefitting quickly. Despite their cynicism, Avril's colleagues were good people who owned up to their mistake. Three months later, they were all prepared to admit that Kevin had changed. He was smiling more, looking more relaxed and they all found it easier to approach him and easier for instance, to take him to the bathroom.

The whole county

Betty was a speech and language therapist working with social services staff in a large day centre. She became interested in and excited by Intensive Interaction. She wanted to start working with one or two of the centre clients using the approach. She started discussing the approach with some members of staff. One of them was interested enough to read a book on the topic, but most of them were relaxed people who liked the sound of working in this way. Some members of staff, though, felt that they could not work in this way.

Betty then involved the manager who was also receptive. She gave her the go-ahead to work with selected clients and three members of staff who were enthusiastic. Betty and her three colleagues held a series of short meetings where they identified who was to be worked with and started documenting what they were about to do.

They didn't start immediately though. Instead they did some careful observation, including starting to shoot videos for baseline purposes. There was also a period of talking to parents and other carers. From these small but carefully planned beginnings, use of the approach has grown and now Intensive Interaction is an important activity in the social services establishments in the county.

Some of the difficulties you might find with acceptance of the approach are not as significant as they would have been some years ago. Intensive Interaction is quite commonly seen around the country in schools, families, social services establishments, health trust establishments and in resources provided by the voluntary sector. Organisations such as the social services authority in the example in the box above will now start wide-ranging schemes to enable their staff to work in this way.

There has also been a shift in the values and philosophies which underpin our work. It is now widely recognised that people with SLD who are still at very early developmental stages have various needs. Staff should give regard to their adult age and status, but not let this stop them from giving the person experiences they can understand and relate to. Having fun, being close to people, 'playing' and even 'romping' are not a contradiction to being an adult. They are part of the range of experiences necessary to the person to have a sense of well-being and to develop relationships.

Further Reading

Phoebe Caldwell works in a similar way to build relationships and improve the lifestyles of challenging individuals with SLD. Her book *Getting in Touch: Ways of Working with People with Severe Learning Disabilities and Extensive Support Needs* (Pavilion) gives lots of examples of practical interaction work and how she starts out with individuals.

SUMMARY

- Start slowly and gently. Give yourself time to think and prepare.

- Choose the person with SLD to start with who is most likely to gain success or whose success is most likely to be significant.

- Doing Intensive Interaction will involve you and colleagues in enjoyable, relaxed and natural interactions with another person. It is good to remember this and stress it to colleagues.

- The technique is a blend of responding naturally and intuitively and deciding consciously from moment to moment.

- Have a period of preparation before starting work.

- Do relaxed, subjective observations of the person you are going to work with.

- It is a good idea to do baseline recordings.

- The team needs to discuss and organise ways of finding quality one-to-one time.

- The team may need to have preparatory discussions to make sure they share understandings about what is being attempted.

Chapter 3
BEING RESPONSIVE

Sections in this chapter:

HOW DO I START?

This section takes you step-by-step through an example of attempting to start Intensive Interaction with a person who will probably be truly difficult to reach. If the person you are thinking about doing Intensive Interaction with already has basic communication abilities and you want to develop them, you may be tempted to move straight to the next chapter. However, it is probably a good idea that you work through the content here also, since this chapter emphasises some basic principles and gives advice on thinking processes which are important at any stage of using the approach.

START WHERE THE OTHER PERSON IS MOST COMFORTABLE

To work through our example, let's say that you are wanting to start working with an isolated teenager with SLD who we shall call Marco. Marco prefers a certain corner of the room and likes to be left alone to sit rocking and twiddling. If other people come too near, he will show signs of distress and may get up and quickly move away until his corner is free again. Marco clearly has all sorts of potential abilities, but frustratingly, he rejects you, sometimes forcefully, when you try to get him to do something new. He may become particularly distressed when asked to leave his corner and work elsewhere. So, the first important principle to start using is that whatever takes place, will happen where Marco is most comfortable, and at ease.

ADJUSTING TO HOW THE PERSON WITH SLD NEEDS YOU TO BE

In fact we would go further and argue that what takes place should happen on **his terms** and with his agreement. It will only happen if he is fully and actively **participating**. He should not be forced to do anything. There should be no demands made of him and no task in these activities. Rather, it is your job to win Marco's attention by using your behaviour cleverly to capture his attention. Clearly, for someone with Marco's attitudes, this can only happen if he is feeling **secure** and **relaxed**, and has developed some trust that your presence near to him is **not threatening.**

For many people who, like Marco, are still at very early stages of understanding the world, the problem for them may be that the world is confusing and threatening. Many people with Marco's lifestyle have autism. what other people around them do, sometimes even the most simple everyday things, can make them feel **fearful** and **anxious**. Many are simply people who are pre-verbal and find being social a very uncomfortable experience, way beyond their understanding.

This is why Intensive Interaction places so much emphasis on everything happening on Marco's terms. The learning experiences will simply not work unless the interactions are on his terms. This might be the main trick for you at first - to make sure that you get the activities right in this way. It can be difficult because in the past you may have been accustomed, for good reasons, to prompting and cajoling Marco, otherwise he does nothing. In using Intensive Interaction, you will be reversing this state of affairs and changing the relationship with him. Part of the idea is to make him powerful, to share power with him.

Where to interact?

The best place to interact is likely to be in the favoured place of the person with SLD, where they are obviously most relaxed and secure, e.g.:

- In a corner of the room
- On the floor
- Standing up by the window
- On a sofa in the living room
- In the swimming pool
- In the soft play room
- In the ball pool
- On two beanbags or a crash mat
- In their bedroom
- During care activities - washing, changing

If what has been said about adjusting to the person with SLD sounds impossible, don't worry, it isn't. It is much easier than you think and once staff get the hang of it, it feels like the most natural thing in the world. It may sound wrong to you too, to work on the person with SLD's terms - like giving in or being weak. You will find you get more comfortable with this too. It may help to think of interaction on the person's own terms as their entitlement. It may also help to think more of negotiation of terms, but with you being more flexible and able to adapt and choosing to do so. One of the problems that Marco has probably always had is that the rest of us have never got this right for him before. We haven't learnt how to have conversations with him on his terms.

Further Reading

The book *Taking Control: Enabling People with Learning Difficulties* (edited by Judith Coupe O'Kane and Beryl Smith, 1994, David Fulton) has useful chapters on this issue of people with SLD having control and personal power.

MAKING YOURSELF AVAILABLE

Hopefully, if you have been doing some of the new, subjective observations recommended in the previous chapter, you will already have started making yourself available to Marco. By this we mean that you will have become a person who he can tolerate being near him. He will not find your presence threatening or anxiety-provoking. You will have started doing things with your face, your voice, your body language, which he finds comfortable and acceptable, even interesting. These things can start to observation stage.

Whilst observing, you don't need to pretend that you are doing anything other than observing. It may be a good idea for Marco to become aware that you are doing something new for him. You may even like to tell him gently; let him know everything that you are doing and why. However, you do need to pay attention to your own style here. You may like to consider just how relaxed you look, or whether you are really a rather brisk and efficient person with quick movements. Try slowing down a bit, a lot of activity may he too much for him, particularly when you are approaching his area of the room.

While you are observing Marco, you may feel at ease sitting upright on a chair, but he may not find your posture appealing and comfortable. Consider somewhere to sit nearby where you can relax, slump out - the floor, a mat, a beanbag, a comfortable chair. Move to this place with good reassuring body language and facial expression. These issues are extremely important. Even though Marco doesn't seem to have much understanding of communication, he may be extremely sensitive to other people's body language and tempo of movement. Probably Marco finds that all the people around him move too quickly and make fierce frightening statements with their body language.

> **What is body language?**
>
> Did you know that what you say is only a very small part of a communication with another person? Research has shown that when we are talking with another person, more than 50% of the communication is by body language. Why not try this out by turning down the sound on the television and realising how much of the communication you understand simply by looking.
>
> Body language is a loose definition of all the non-verbal things that we do: gesture, facial expression, eye contact, posture, distance, appearance. All of us take in visual messages from other people in a constant stream, second-by-second. We are very good at analysing these messages for meanings, but the skills for doing this tend to be sub-conscious. We don't usually think about it consciously.

One of the skills that staff using Intensive Interaction well gradually develop, is the ability to manage their **body language** and to use it powerfully and deliberately. In order to do this, they may develop an ability to use body language more consciously than people usually do. Part of the process of being available to Marco may well be to gradually develop this ability to think a bit more about your body language and deliberately 'talk' to Marco with it. You may need to 'say' things like: "Everything's safe, I'm safe, I'm really paying attention to how you are feeling;" or "Here I am, everything's fine"; or "I'm here for you, on your terms, I'll go away as soon as you've had enough of me."

(As you develop your ability with body language, you may well find yourself becoming more and more effective if you work with people who have challenging behaviour. Good defusers of incidents of **challenging behaviour** are people who use their body language effectively).

RESPONDING TO SIGNALS

RESPOND INSTANTLY TO SIGNALS OF NEGATIVITY

There is a further, vital aspect of making yourself available. You need to be prepared to make yourself **unavailable** as soon as Marco tells you this. Whilst observing, but particularly whilst trying to get an interaction started, you must watch Marco's body language carefully. You are particularly watching for signals of **negativity**. If Marco does anything which you suspect is telling you to go, or that he doesn't like something, then you need to go, or stop the activity, instantly.

> **Signalling**
>
> This word will occur frequently from now on in this book. 'Signalling' refers to the deliberate things people do to send messages by smiling, nodding, moving a hand, their shoulders, an elbow etc. Potentially, people can signal with any part of their body, though most of us in society share a set of standard forms of signalling that we all know.

Responding to signals of negativity is a basic **principle** of Intensive Interaction at all levels. Remember, we are trying to get the person with SLD to have the activity on their terms. We are trying to help them learn how to enjoy other people, to share **personal power** in the situation, to participate fully and enjoyably. So, obviously, when they have had enough, the interaction should stop. Trying to keep going when the person has had enough may leave them with a negative memory of the experience and make it less likely they will want to do it again. Giving the person with SLD the power to control the situation makes it more likely that they will take part, and more likely that they will keep going with confidence.

For Marco, it is essential that we give him this power. That is to say, that we give Marco a sense of **security** that he might not have ever had before, by moving away when we sense he is telling us to. By giving him this ability to control us through our responsiveness, we make it more likely that he will feel confident about letting us stay near, because he is assured we will go when he has had enough.

For Marco, the issue is an extreme one, he is extremely isolated by his anxiety. Many other people with SLD will not be as fearful of other people being near as this. However, in general terms, this principle of responding to negative signals from the other person applies throughout Intensive Interaction activities. When the activities have grown and developed, it may be that our response to a negative signal is simply to change position or change the activity, and that may be enough.

TUNING-IN

Naturally, a basic skill for you, the communication partner, is to observe finely enough to pick up these signals. This process of 'tuning-in' to Marco's body language, to his noises, to his behaviour and lifestyle, should have intensified during the observation stage. That is why we place so much emphasis on subjective observation. The subjective observation helps you truly to get to know the perhaps tiny things that Marco does which are a communication or a possible communication. In a sense, there is nothing unusual or 'special' about doing this for Marco. We have already made the point that more than 50% of interpersonal communication is non-verbal. Watch all people talking to each other. See how carefully and minutely we scrutinise each other during conversation. We are all very good at picking up tiny signals of meaning.

With Marco the only difference is that his face and body movements may be quite 'idiosyncratic' - quite original and different to him. Actually, it could be the case that for all of his life, Marco has made intentional communication signals, but because these signals are so different, so unique to him, other people failed to notice or interpret them. This can be the case even when we are very experienced at our work, even when we have known someone like Marco for a long time. Many people with SLD but with limited communication abilities make deliberate attempts at communication which go unnoticed. Worse still, these attempts may be noticed but not responded to. Part of the 'art' of being a communication partner, is to tune yourself in to the unique way that Marco behaves and potentially sends signals. The next part is, of course, to find ways to respond which are effective for Marco.

It may also be the case that Marco doesn't make intentional signals. However, he may have many little things which he does which can **potentially** become intentional communications if those things are responded to effectively. Part of the

People with PMLD

It can be difficult to know the communication abilities of a person with PMLD. If this person has profound intellectual disabilities, it may well be that they do not make intentional communication signals. However, this person may have many movements or noises which, with your assistance, might become intentional signals. It is a matter of selecting things the person does which seem like a communication to you, and responding as if it is meaningful - and doing this frequently and consistently. Obviously, as you are doing this, you stay tuned-in for any realisation you may get that the person is now starting to do something deliberately, to signal at you. You also need to stay tuned to the possibility that your assigned meaning was wrong and needs to be altered.

On the other hand, a person may have more communication ability than we realise, but we fail to see their signals amongst many uncontrolled movements. They may signal with a flick of a toe, a finger, a particular head movement, a nudge of a thigh, a bobbing movement of the whole body - anything in fact. Our job is to be sensitive to this and pick it up, for each individual person. If the signals are not responded to, the person may give up trying to be a communicator.

observation and tuning-in process is to recognise these things and become familiar with them. You don't have to write a list, though some notes may help. It is better to be tuned-in by being deeply, subjectively familiar with them.

This process of being tuned-in continues throughout Intensive Interaction activities at all levels. It is another of the basic principles for the technique.

Again, we would emphasise that in a general sense, there is nothing unusual or 'special' about this for people with SLD. The only difference is the effort we make to learn the other person's way of signalling. Actually, we may go so far as to say that where we don't do this, or where we have failed to learn how to communicate with each individual person, **we** are a significant aspect of that person's disability.

Further Reading

Eye to Eye: How People Interact. Peter Marsh. Oxford: Guild Publishing 1988. This is a large-format extensively illustrated book which puts knowledge on human interaction into an easily-accessible form.
See What I Mean (BILD/Mencap) A useful resource helping you to make sense of when and how to interpret the idiosyncratic signals of people with PMLD.

Ideally, early communication activities take place best when the two people are reasonably close to each other, sharing personal space. This makes it easier for the two people to read very tiny signals, or hear tiny noises, or to exchange physical contact.

For many of the people with SLD you spend time with, this is not a problem. You may already have such a relationship with the person that being physically close is easy and routine. The person may have knowledge and ability sufficient to not be concerned, in the way that Marco is, about other people's presence. You may already have established the occasional playful interaction with the person. The person may be someone with PMLD who

Don't forget - approach sensitively

Remember to make yourself available. Being available means using care in the speed of your approach and managing your body language so that you are a person that the other person can feel comfortable with. Slow down, take your time, relax, respond and enjoy. These are the watchwords.

has long become accustomed to other people's proximity, if only to receive care. With Marco however, being close to him is not easy, so it may be necessary at first to start interacting from a distance.

RESPONDING BY CELEBRATING WHAT IS NEW OR WELCOME

FINDING BEHAVIOURS TO CELEBRATE

What you need to go on to do next is to try out responses to the other person's behaviours. You may already have some good ideas about which behaviours from your observations. On the other hand, you may not have any fixed ideas about which behaviours you will focus on, but you feel confident about being there and trying things out, really working 'off the cuff'.

Engagement

Human beings learn best when the learning activity engages them. What we mean by this is that the activity stimulates the intellect and the emotions and becomes the most interesting thing in a person's mind at that moment.   A student at university is a sophisticated learner who can be engaged by a learning activity for extended periods. In the early stages of work with Marco, we might be doing well if what we do engages him for three seconds.

One of the problems faced by the people with SLD who are the focus of this book, is that previously we may not have before made serious enough attempts to engage them. We might have tried to get them to take part in all sorts of activities, but without getting them truly engaged. Consequently, though they apparently 'took part' in the activity, they may not have actually learnt anything.

Learning to be engaged by something somebody else has on offer is one of the basic things learnt during Intensive Interaction, and one of the foundations of all other learning.

To follow through our example, Marco might murmur "hum". In response, you would need to celebrate, perhaps with a gentle laugh, "huuuuum".   What happens next would involve you looking for any sign that what you did in your response caused interest. You would need to continually check whether what you did gets Marco to become engaged with you, however briefly. You might think of this as looking for any sign that you can 'light him up'.

To put it basically, at this stage you are experimenting with your responses to things that the other person does. As you try out your celebrations, you need to keep on looking for possible responses from the person with SLD to what you just did. We might say you are looking for feedback and you will use that feedback to help you decide what to do next. The main feedback you are looking for is any sign of interest or engagement.

Remember that there is no limit to the things that you might do at this stage. The main idea to get across to the person with SLD is that: your behaviour is important, I like your behaviour, if you do things I will respond. The boxes on the next page attempt to give a feel for the range of possibilities. The boxes only provide examples for illustration. We cannot hope to describe the range of things which are possible between two people.

So be relaxed, be creative, enjoy attempting to use your behaviour to celebrate what the other person does and light them up. Of course, remember too that it is not necessary to celebrate everything. There may be things that the other person does that you may not feel comfortable about and certainly would not wish to imitate or join in with. That's fine. Respond to and celebrate the things you do feel comfortable about, but don't expect them to be conventional communication behaviours.

TRY NOT TO BOMBARD

Remember too, that you should try hard not to bombard the other person with your behaviour. Yes, be happy, be fun, celebrate the other person's behaviour, but make the tempo of your behaviour like their tempo, have pauses, pauses which give both of you time to think. You need pauses to watch for signals; your communication partner needs pauses to think about signals.

In our example, Marco has vocalised "hum" and you respond, "huuuuum", in a slightly laughing voice and turn your head slightly to look sideways smiling. As you do this you are tuning-in, looking carefully for any sign that Marco might have registered what you just did and become attracted by it. He has been sitting rocking and flicking, but now you see him pause slightly - there is just a moment when he is still, his head slightly turned so that it seems as if he is listening. You respond to this: "Okay, was that good?" laughing softly.

You and Marco have probably just had a meaningful interaction - a dialogue. We can draw a map of it that looks like this:

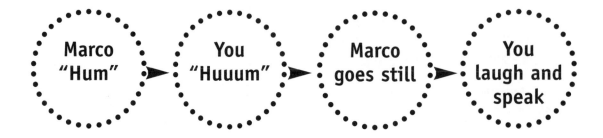

Where shall I stand or sit?

It is a good idea when trying to interact with many people with SLD, to position yourself deliberately so that your eye level is below theirs. This can increase the confidence and sense of security for people who are anxious about their personal space.

Additionally, for people with PMLD, who are perhaps wheelchair users, it simply may make the whole thing easier for them if you have positioned yourself so that your face is easily available.

For those of you who spend time with very young children, it is imperative that for most of the day, your face is available. This may mean being prepared to spend a lot of time on the floor or crouching. Remember, these children cannot learn to look at your face if your face is up in the sky.

Even with that little burst of behaviour of about three seconds between you and Marco, you can see the beginnings of meaningful communication - a turn-taking sequence of two turns each. You used your behaviour to help Marco be aware of the communication of another person and to start to rehearse turn-taking. While this is a very small beginning, it is a beginning, and it provides all sorts of possibilities. If Marco is okay about you staying near, then the next few moments may be taken up with watching to find another behaviour which you can celebrate, or perhaps Marco will do the "hum" again and you can have a go at repeating the little burst as before.

This may be enough for a first session. Indeed, with somebody as anxious as Marco, it may take a considerable number of attempts even to achieve this. So, it is important to be patient, or better still, to have helpful and appropriate expectations. Having the right expectations is better than being patient, it is less stressful. For Marco, the expectation might be that as he has become adult without learning to communicate or to be comfortable with people being near him, changing this will take time. It will take time to get to know him and to experience small successes like the one illustrated above. By adjusting your expectations, it becomes easier to recognise and create gradual progress.

If the people you are working with have profound and multiple disabilities, there can be complications due to their difficulty with controlling their movements. You may have difficulty identifying responses amongst uncontrolled movements. It will perhaps take time and tuning-in to start to identify any deliberate signals.

Gemma - a little girl with PMLD

Gemma's physical disabilities are considerable. She is silent, moving very little - she simply doesn't seem to be able to make any controlled movements. Her eyes do not seem to change to denote recognition when another person comes near.

Her teachers, however, suspect that she may have more awareness than she is able to show. For a few weeks, Astrid has been attempting to start interacting. Right now, Astrid is lying on the mat next to Gemma, with her head raised into Gemma's line of sight. Astrid is totally focused, murmuring a running commentary now and again. She is also tuned-in for Gemma's blinks. The instant that Gemma blinks, Astrid raises her head even more and laughs explosively but gently. "Yeh Gem, I liked that, I did."

Astrid's colleague Sue is kneeling a few feet away recording with a video camera. After school, Astrid and Sue will watch the tape several times, to help them decide whether any of Gemma's blinks, or anything else she might have done, were deliberate and intentional.

What do we respond to?

Any possible thing that the other person does that you feel comfortable with, e.g.

- **Vocalisations** - grunts, murmurs, humming, hissing, hooting, all voice noises. In infant development parents are very keen to respond to all vocalisations.

- **Other noises** made with the mouth - clicks, saliva swishing, blowing, smacking lips, tongue waggling etc.

- **Other noises** - slapping or tapping parts of the body, slapping or tapping furniture or walls, foot tapping or stamping, clapping or hand rubbing etc.

- **Movements** - hand arm movements, rocking, swaying or other movements of the trunk, if you have the energy, quite physical movement around the room, movements of the legs and feet, head bobbing, reaching out, etc.

- **Facial expressions** - smiles, grimaces, mouth opening and closing, eyebrow movements, blinks, momentary eye contact, face simply turned slightly toward you, etc.

- **Physical contact** - pats, taps, reaching to hold you, etc.

- **Stereotyped behaviour** - many people with SLD have a rich and organised range of repetitive and rhythmic behaviour they enjoy. One possibility is to try joining-in.

How do we respond?

As imaginatively and creatively as you like, e.g.:

- **By imitating** - by providing a recognisably similar imitation of what the other person just did, but combined with clear signals of enjoyment from you.

- **By joining in** - joining in will usually mean an extended response, e.g. joining-in with rocking or clapping, again combined with other responses, particularly of course signals of fun and enjoyment.

- **By saying something** - a good celebration might be to simply say something which is obviously approving, e.g. "yeah", "alright", "oh yes, that's clever", "that's a good noise" and so on.

- **By being dramatic** - a momentary behaviour from the other person is rewarded by something gently 'explosive' from you - a sudden upright movement with a delighted face, a sudden draw back with an expression of mock fear or horror, a vocalisation - "Hah!"

- **By non-verbal responses** - smiling, widening eyes, anything you do with your face, nodding or moving your head, any obviously significant body language you use as a response.

- **By running commentary** - "Hey yeah, you're pleased to see me, I know."

It may be that be that the person with PMLD has not yet reached the stage of deliberate intentional behaviour. In this case, you need to respond to certain movements or sounds the person makes as if they are social or communicative. If you do this over a period of time, with intensity and consistency, it will help the person to realise that something that they do accidently, is actually causing you to do something. They may then get the idea and start doing it deliberately. In this way we foster the development of intentionality.

FOSTERING INTENTIONAL COMMUNICATION

With your responses to the other person, at first you are attempting to do two things:

1. Recognise and respond to anything you think the person did that was an intentional attempt at communicating with you.

2. Respond deliberately to something the person does which isn't intentionally a communication, as if it was a communication. By doing this regularly, you help them to realise that they can have an effect and cause you to respond.

WHAT ABOUT PEOPLE WHO ARE DEAF/BLIND?

Some of the people with SLD with extreme needs in the areas of social and communication development will have additional sensory impairments; they may be deaf and blind. This can be intimidating when we think about how we start to interact and how we help the person to become aware of our responses.

The first thing to be said is that few people are completely deaf or completely blind. It is always a good idea to continue to explore ways in which the person you are working with can learn to use these channels of communication. Certainly, it has been a frequently-heard comment from the communication partners of people with visual disabilities, that the more they interacted with them, the better their eyesight became and the more they used it. Of course, it is quite unlikely that using Intensive Interaction improved a person's eyesight. What is more probable, is that as they become more aware of, and interested in, the concept of communicating with other people, they become more motivated to use the visual ability they have always possessed.

The second important point concerns a point of principle, or even of human rights. If a person is totally blind and deaf, how are we, the staff or carers, going to give this person fulfilling experiences of being with other people and having relationships? How are we going to communicate with this person? There seems to be only one channel of communication and that is through physical contact.

Physical contact can seem to be a problematic issue in our work. As we have already discussed, people with SLD, particularly people who are pre-verbal, may often have a desire to make physical contact with the people around them. We may frequently question whether it is appropriate to give it, particularly if the person is adult. We discuss these issues further in Chapter Six. One point to be made here, however, is that people with SLD

Communication - a human right?

Human beings are different from other animals in the way in which we communicate in such a rich and complex way. Communicating seems to be central to being human. Being able to communicate gives us the ability to have relationships, friendships, to know the joy and fulfillment of human interaction. It is that important. When people have communication difficulties, it frequently has a negative effect on their well-being and behaviour.

We would say that for people with SLD, developing their communication ability is the most important issue in their lives. It is so important that we can view it virtually as a right. We, the staff or carers, have an absolute duty to do our best to supply the experiences necessary for this development.

frequently do not just desire physical contact, they need it, for very good, human reasons. We think they should have it. Best of all, they should have it from responsible carers working together in teams, being properly managed and supervised, working within a framework of policy, guidelines and safeguard provided by a thoughtful employer. These days, you are much more likely to see this state of affairs than you were ten years ago.

If a person is totally deaf and blind, the staff working with that person must be prepared to give rich social experience through physical contact. It is possible to do Intensive Interaction sessions with a person, with the main channel of communication being touch. The principles will remain the same as outlined previously in this chapter.

THE MOST RESPONSIVE PIECE OF EQUIPMENT

EQUIPMENT

In our work, we will frequently employ ingenious equipment, toys and technology in an attempt to occupy, interest or engage people who have difficulty interacting with the world. We have sensory rooms or Snoezelen rooms which may have electronic sound and light equipment. Some of this equipment incorporates switches and is designed to be 'interactive' - a person can learn that if I press this thing here, something interesting happens. In schools it is common to find plastic or wooden activity centres, which click, rattle or ting when buttons are pressed. The use of personal computers and other micro-technology offers an even greater range and variety of interesting things which can happen when buttons are pressed or various switches are activated.

All of these types of equipment are useful and successful with people with SLD because they all provide opportunity for the person to play with and explore cause and effect - I do something and it causes something else to happen. Exploring cause and effect offers enormous potential for interest and for affirming our sense of ourselves as effective - as able to make things happen in the world. This equipment, then, is very useful and can provide great enjoyment and benefit to people with SLD.

CONTINGENT RESPONDING

However, let us consider what it is the equipment is designed to do. It is designed to respond contingently when somebody does certain things to it. That is to say, the response from the piece of equipment will be obviously and directly related to what the person just did. It will be interesting because it provides opportunities to explore cause and effect. All these items of equipment are definitely worth having for those reasons. Nonetheless, it can be easy to forget that the best piece of equipment, the most flexible, sensitive, intelligent and creative tool that can be offered to a person with SLD, is another human being who is being responsive. It is you! You can find endlessly imaginative ways to offer yourself to a person with SLD so that they become aware of, and confident to explore, cause and effect. Better still, with you the person will be able to explore social cause and effect. That is, the idea that I do something and it causes somebody else to do something. This is another way of thinking about what we are trying to achieve with Intensive Interaction.

You can achieve everything that a piece of equipment can and a lot more. You are more flexible in what you can do. You are more sensitive to the person's behaviours and intentions. You are more able to tune-in and more able to develop and extend what is taking place. This is not a reason to abandon all that interactive equipment, but it is a reason to value the human resource. Playing with an activity centre or the lights in the sensory room can help the person with SLD develop cause and effect, but playing with you, with or without the activity centre/sensory room, can help them develop cause and effect and other vital social and communication abilities.

Further Reading

For further discussion of the importance of being responsive and ideas about how to extend this to the environment generally, we recommend Jean Ware's book: *Creating a Responsive Environment for People with Profound and Multiple Learning Difficulties* (1996, David Fulton).

TROUBLESHOOTING

What about if the person with SLD is really passive and nothing seems to work?

- Try doing less of everything. It may be that this person is so reserved in their preferences and lifestyle, that everything you have tried so far is not stimulating because it is still too complicated. Try reducing your responses in quantity, looking for occasional tactical moments to make a response. Try responding with 'less' behaviour, making what you do less noisy or exciting, less intense.

- Perhaps it is a good idea to go back to a 'quiet' period, where you don't even try to make responses and light the person up, but simply spend time sharing space, being near them. Something may develop from that, even an initiation from the person with SLD, because they have become more comfortable and they feel more secure with your style.

- Maybe there are responses that you haven't noticed. Try videoing some of your attempts at responses. Watch the video very carefully to see if there are things that the person with SLD is doing that you haven't noticed in real-life.

- Try being more alert to opportunities to respond to unintentional behaviours, such as the person sneezing or coughing, and responding to these in a playful way, as if they were social behaviours.

What do you do if the person with SLD is highly active - continually on the move?
- The first and most obvious tactic is to employ the principles of joining them in their world and to move around with them in order to create shared activities. This can be very effective, though there are obvious difficulties. It is a good idea not to attempt this in a large room such as a gymnasium - a smaller room or soft-play area may be more advisable. You might like to give the activity to the younger or more energetic members of staff.

- Whilst attempting to start interacting in this way, it is of course still the theme that you will be trying to create enjoyable moments of face-to-face, or moments of eye-contact and shared pleasure, gradually at first and then extending these moments. Playful physical contact can definitely be helpful, especially if this contributes to creating moments of stillness for you both. One of the purposes of the sessions is to extend these moments of stillness.

- You may prefer not to rush around with the person, but rather move at your own pace, positioning yourself cleverly in their line of sight as they move. This can be developed into a tease or anticipation game with the aim of extending dramatic moments or a sequence of interactions.

He 'lights-up' and enjoys it for twenty seconds, but then doesn't want to know.
- Again, try doing less. What you are doing in your responses may be very enjoyable at first, but perhaps you are so extrovert and exuberant that the other person is overwhelmed by your behaviour and has to 'shut down'. It is a very common difficulty that staff have, simply putting into

the interaction more behaviour than is needed. Once again, it may be helpful to shoot a video and watch yourself.

- Perhaps that is what this person's interactions are like at this point in time. Try relaxing and enjoying them for what they are now and give it more time instead of worrying about it.

Joining-in or imitating isn't working, she just keeps moving away.

- Perhaps she isn't ready to take part in interactions yet and may need more preparation time with you being nearby, sharing space and time whilst she builds up a sense of security.

- Perhaps you are too close and things might work better if you try interacting from a few feet further away.

- You could try taking the first turn. Rather than simply waiting for the person with SLD to do something you respond to, try starting by doing something yourself and see if that produces a response to which you can then respond.

SUMMARY

- Being responsive begins with you adjusting to how the person with SLD needs you to be.

- Being responsive involves making yourself available.

- You need to respond to the person's signals, however small or difficult to read.

- You need to become skilled and sensitive with body language.

- Respond to any intended or potential communication or social initiation.

- Respond by celebrating new and welcome behaviours.

- You are the best and most responsive piece of equipment there is.

Chapter 4
INTERACTIVE GAMES

Sections in this chapter:

In Chapter Three we gave some practical guidance on how you need to behave and respond as an effective Communication partner in Intensive Interaction. In this chapter we describe the possible content of the interactions between you and the person with SLD. We talk about the qualities of the interactions that makes them good for fostering a relationship between you and good for fostering communication development. We talk about the interactions as interactive games as we think this is most accurate and most helpful.

THE VALUE OF INTERACTIVE GAMES

If you are working with, or caring for, a young child with SLD, the need for playing interactive games may seem very obvious to you. Indeed, the desire to play interactive games may also come naturally to you. This may be less the case the more severe the child's impairments, the less typical their behaviours, or the more anxious or uncomfortable you are. Your earliest attempts at interactive games may have gone unrewarded and you may have been put off or become awkward in your interactive style. If the child has autistic difficulties it may seem that interactive game is the last thing they want or need. Difficulties with interactive game-playing does not mean tat interactive game is no longer relevant - rather that it is just that - difficult.

It may not always be popular among staff working with adults with learning difficulties to think about playing with them, but interactive games and play have an important role in the development of communication and social abilities for older people too. We can try to make this sound more age-appropriate by talking about interactive exchanges or interactive sequences. However, this may then mean that we ignore an important central issue in the lives of many adult people with SLD - they may like interactive play and benefit enormously from it. It may also mean that we ignore the important playful element of the interactive exchange.

Interactive games are effective for people with SLD because of their key features:

- games are joint activities with mutual involvement (which help to establish common references and shared meanings)

- games involve repetition (which allows for repeated practice without boredom and provides predictable, secure activities)

- games involve alternate turn-taking (which means opportunities for learning and practising one of the most fundamental rules of conversation - taking turns)

- games are intrinsically motivating because of their intrinsic fun (which helps to ensure that they are played often with positive associations)

- games provide opportunities for solving problems (which means opportunities for applying thinking skills, involving effort but not stress)

Further Reading

If you are interested in reading more on this topic there are a number of academic papers on the importance and nature of interactive games including:

Field, T. (1979) 'Games parents play with normal and high-risk infants', Child Psychiatry and Human Development, 10, 1, 41-48.

Hodapp, R.M. & Goldfield, E.C. (1983) 'The use of mother-infant games as therapy with delayed children', Early Child Development and Care, 13, 17-32.

Roy McConkey's chapter, 'Interaction: the name of the game' in Beryl Smith's (1987) *Interactive Approaches to the Education of Children with Severe Learning Difficulties*. (Westhill College)

The problem with the notion of games is that it might fit with our notion of babies and children and not with our notion of adults with SLD. In this scenario it is easy to under-estimate the value of games as 'work' or as serious intervention with countless benefits for the individual's development. Games can be dismissed as for children only, when we know that people of all ages play games and benefit from them. Adults in everyday situations can be extended (cognitively, socially, physically) through games or they can simply gain through stress reduction. It is for people at the early stages of development, whatever their age, however, that there is a particularly good match between developmental needs and basic interactive game-playing.

Fortunately, we are moving away from a time when adults who have SLD were viewed only from the point of view of their chronological ages. Staff everywhere are increasingly accepting that whilst it is important to give proper regard to a person's age and adult status, they have other needs too. That person will have an emotional and psychological 'age' and a level of communication ability which also needs to be addressed.

Further Reading

Our views on the issue of age-appropriateness are outlined in a book on various controversial issues surrounding work with people with SLD. Other views on age-appropriateness are also included in the book:

Whose Choice? Contentious Issues for those Working with People with Learning Difficulties, Coupe O'Kane & Goldbart (eds) (1996). London: David Fulton.

Chapter by Nind & Hewett   'When age-appropriateness isn't appropriate' and chapter by Grove, Porter & Park   'Ages and Stages: What is Appropriate Behaviour?'. Beryl Smith reviews the arguments in her chapter 'Discussion: Age-Appropriate or Developmentally Appropriate Activities?'

PREPARING FOR INTERACTIVE GAMES

Two important features of parent-baby games is that they provide what the baby needs now, and they build for later development. In fact, as illustrated in some of the examples appearing in this book, the games themselves develop as the child develops. Interactive games are helpful because they provide a secure situation for the baby, or the person with SLD, to perform at their best. The game situation provides enjoyable motivation and the lack of stress means that complicated learning takes place almost without the person realising it. In fact, a person with SLD will be working at, if you like, maximum performance during these games, but will not be doing so in response to demand by the member of staff. Thus, skills that cannot yet be performed out of the game context are possible here, because the social environment of the game is so supportive. The game context is important for the adult or staff member to perform at their best too. Here the stress of tasks is taken away for you too and you get to know the person you are playing with as an active and likeable companion with whom you can spend time.

We have already outlined the importance of preparation and observation for getting started with Intensive Interaction. Those sections of the book apply to the business of establishing interactive games as well as to 'accessing' the person with SLD. It may also be worth thinking about some particular strategies with interactive games. Setting the stage can be important for cueing in to the game. Use of props, such as a familiar ball to roll back and forward or a favoured piece of cloth under which you hide, can indicate to the person that you are about to play. This can be particularly important if the person with learning difficulties also has sensory impairments. Anticipating the game can get you both feeling relaxed and playful. Setting the scene might also involve organising the room in a particular way, or positioning yourself opposite the communication partner on the floor, for example.

Having set the scene, you need to establish joint attention. This might involve bouncing the ball yourself a few times before rolling it to the other person. It might involve calling the person's name or singing a rhyme. Attention-gaining devices related to the games both trigger attention, and cue the person into the game about to be played. With attention gained the game can unfold, but the strategy remains to provide the playful context in which the communication partner can explore and practice their skills. There is no place in game-playing for heavy direction or an atmosphere of demands.

WHAT MAKES A GOOD INTERACTIVE GAME?

We play interactive games because we find them enjoyable and rewarding. In some senses, therefore, all interactive games are good for social development as they reinforce the enjoyment of being with, and interacting with, other people. Not all games, however, are equally valuable for fostering progression of social abilities, quality communication, and cognitive development. If we are to make play successful for people with severe learning difficulties, therefore, we need to understand what makes some interactive games better than others.

There follows a list of early interactive games played by more than 50% of parents and children in a study by Tiffany Field (1979).

- *'Tell me a story'* The most frequently played game in Field's classic study. This involves the parent asking the baby to tell a story, and the parent responding to the baby's vocalisations, as if they are the words of the story. The parent provides the words and the reactions to the story.

- *'I'm gonna get you'* A game in which the parent threatens in an exagerrated and playful way, with wide-eyed expression and dramatic hand-poising to pounce and tickle. This usually elicits laughter in response.

- *'Walking fingers' or 'creepie crawlies'* A game in which the adult walks her fingers spider-like up the baby's body, again often culminating in laughter.

- *'So big'* A game involving stretching the baby's arms upward - as if to make him taller and commenting "so big" etc.

- *'Pat-a-cake'* A rhyme with clapping action.

- *Peek-a-boo'* The classic hide and appear again game with anticipation and climax.

How many of these are familiar to you? What would you add from your own experience? And most importantly, what is it about these games that means they are played by so many?

We could list dozens more frequently played games. It is probably unhelpful however, to use a list as your guiding framework for starting games, as every individual, or pair, or group of individuals, have their own preferences for the content of their games. Indeed, the best games are child-initiated which undermines the need for staff to have a list of games. It is the features of the games that make them effective that we need to understand so that we can steer, extend and enhance the potential of any interactive play situation.

EFFECTIVE GAMES ARE STIMULATING

When the baby is small, or the individual with learning difficulties is developmentally young, the games have to be stimulating to be effective. A characteristic of many of the games listed above is that they combine different sorts of stimulation - visual, auditory, tactile and kinaesthetic (that is, they involve looking, listening, touch and moving).

Georgina

Georgina is four and she has severe learning difficulties. Other members of her integrated nursery school find her unrewarding as a companion or play partner. Her facial expression tends to be unchanging and she is mostly passive. Her nursery nurse, Jane, has been briefed in the principles of Intensive Interaction and she wants to get some fun going between them. She approaches Georgina who is lying on her back with her knees bent up and feet flat on the floor. Rather than move her to come and play, Jane assumes a similar posture on the floor beside her. Georgina fidgets and Jane playfully imitates. Georgina's knees flop out to the sides, so do Jane's. Georgina straightens one leg into the air, so does Jane. Georgina is quickly aware that she is controlling Jane and sees the fun in this. Soon an elaborate game of leg movements and knee tapping evolves. It is more of a game than a kind of dance movement routine because Jane is behind Georgina in her timing, because she adds some sound effects, and because she brings chuckles of laughter to the exchange.

EFFECTIVE GAMES COME FROM RESPONDING

Games don't have to be highly structured and rule-governed, though they inevitably have some structure and negotiated rules. As we showed in the previous chapter, games can develop from your responsiveness to the person with SLD. By responding in a relaxed, playful manner an interactive game may develop. The fact that this game stems from the person with SLD's own activity means that it is likely to be meaningful and fun for them. By making sure our activity is based upon the other person's activity we create game-like turns where they would otherwise not have existed.

EFFECTIVE GAMES HAVE RHYTHM

Responding can become game-like by adding rhythm. Think of all the nursery rhymes and baby games you know and consider the rhythm in them. This is what helps to make them familiar and what gives them structure.

EFFECTIVE GAMES HAVE ANTICIPATION

Now think of anticipation in other baby games like 'peek-a-boo' and 'round-and-round-the -garden' and 'I'm gonna get you...'. These are brilliant for gaining and holding the child's attention. The sheer anticipation of the playful peek or tickle brings in the adrenalin so that the heart beats faster and the body and mind are prepared for stimulation. Such games can be highly arousing and we know that they can lead to over-excitement. This is why these games can be used to help people with SLD regulate their level of arousal. We need arousal to peak so that we learn how to bring it down again, how to cope by looking away or ending the game. Without rehearsing the arousal regulating mechanisms the social world can be permanently over-stimulating and, as such, something to be avoided.

EFFECTIVE GAMES HAVE REPETITION

If you watch parents and babies playing you will notice that they almost never do anything just once. The nature of their games is such that various turns or bursts of activity are repeated within a sequence and the sequence itself is often repeated over and over. The number of repetitions is usually dictated by the amount of fun each generates. This, in turn, is linked with how important the game is for the individual's current level of development. We can illustrate with the example of the game of rolling a ball to and fro across the floor from mother to baby (taken from Hodapp & Goldfield, 1983). At first, when the mother has to take the ball back herself, the game is repeated few times. When the baby begins to roll the ball back himself, the game is played over and over until the skill is required and the sense of achievement well-established. Then, when the game loses its novelty value and no longer needs so much practice, the repetitions become fewer again.

Matty

Matty is five and has autism and learning difficulties. He quite likes rough and tumble games and other playful physical contact but he rarely looks at people's faces or shares in communication. Kate, his teacher, pulls him to sit on her lap whispering in his ear, "this is the way the gentlemen ride". Matty relaxes and waits, expecting the familiar rhyme. She begins chanting the rhyme and in a steady rhythm jiggles him "clip-clop-clip-clop". With each verse the rhythm remains but the chorus "clip-clop" varies in speed and intensity. She judges whether the stimulus needs to be made greater or lesser by his responses, and she pauses to await the look (that will come in time) before following through the fun part of the rhyme each time.

Repetition makes the games meaningful and familiar (as does basing games on the child's activity). The highly repetitive, simple, even stereotyped roles assumed in games make them manageable even for the least developed of thinkers. Games are only fun if you know, to some extent, what's coming next. They seem to make it legitimate to do things over and over again. This makes them ideal for rehearsing communication. It is through repeated use that one learns that a tilt of the head signals a desire to play, that dipping forward signals desire for another turn, and so on.

EFFECTIVE GAMES INVOLVE TAKING TURNS

We have noted that games are good for rehearsing the skills needed for later conversation - notably taking turns. It is easy to think of the turn-taking involved in a board-game like ludo, but turn-taking starts much earlier in very basic games involving two players. (The earliest turn-taking involves jiggling the baby in pauses between sucking in feeding.) Almost all of the games described so far have an element of 'you do something - I do something'. At the earliest stages we create turns in our games by interweaving our activity into the activity of the other person. The desire to take turns is not present at this stage, but the feeling of turns is artificially created. The 'tell me a story game' is a good example of this. The adult creates the dialogue by interspersing activity with comments. Basic imitation sequences can become turn-taking in the same way. The child begins by just doing their own thing, but we can make it feel two-way by deliberately imitating some of the things the child does.

In many of the well-known rhymes, such as 'this little piggy' turns are created in a different way. The adult still creates the turn-taking but here s/he is doing most of the activity and pauses for a look or for taking breath or any potential response before going on the next line of the rhyme. The fact that the game is played over and over means that the child knows when the pauses come and some kind of stilling or looking or vocalising is almost inevitable. Turns don't have to take the form of words or similar actions. It is the alternating input and the shared attention that is crucial.

ENDING INTERACTIVE GAMES

When we do training sessions on Intensive Interaction we are sometimes asked how to end interactions. In the early stages when you are seizing an opportunity to respond and create a few seconds of togetherness this is not an issue. By the time you have established a good repertoire of interactive games together though, some of these may be so enjoyable that it is hard to know when to stop. We can even become irritated with the person with SLD when they want to go on and on, or when they demand an interaction at a time that is not convenient to us. We have to remind ourselves that knowing about ending interactions (and when to have them) will not be automatic for people with SLD - they have to learn it - we have to teach them.

Some games, especially those with lots of anticipation and tease, culminate in a climax of laughter which brings them to a lively but obvious close. More often games peak and trough many times and we may need to choose a good moment to bring the thing to a close. It is important, we think, that we choose a trough for this, that is, a moment of lower arousal. This is less likely to leave the person feeling frustrated and more likely to help them to see how they can end the game themselves.

We have worked with people who have had no problems with ending games, they have simply walked off or turned away when they have had enough and we have respected this. On occasions we have known people who have ended a game with an act of aggression. While this is unusual it is also upsetting and leads us to question ourselves as skilled communication partners. It may be that for these individuals, they don't know a better way yet, of telling us they've had enough and we need to help them with this.

Ending interactive games takes thought and care just as starting them does. The guiding principles of being observant and responding to signals, and of using intuition and reflection, are just as important at this stage as at the beginning. On a note of caution, we remind you that more than anything you want the person with SLD to be left feeling good about themselves and about you and the interaction; you want them to want to come back for more. Ending too abruptly, or attempting to draw out the interactive game so that it lasts uncomfortably long, will work against you and this important aim.

Malcolm

Malcolm is a young man with SLD and challenging behaviour who has become a fun partner in interactive game. He enjoys imitation sequences based on pulling funny faces, hand play and big gestures with his arms. He laughs at staff attempts to follow his sequences and sustains joint attention for long periods. Sessions could have gone on for longer than his teachers had time for and they sometimes had to end the game and move on to work with another student. On some of the best occasions of quality interactive game, Malcolm would react to the game being over by throwing a chair. This was an unwelcome return to earlier difficult behaviours and a real cause for concern. The threat of injury to others was sufficient to almost make the class team want to stop interacting with Malcolm altogether. If he didn't have the interaction he didn't throw the furniture. However, they were experienced enough to know that this solution was no solution as it was through the interactions that they had got to know Malcolm and enabled him to develop lots of new abilities.

They decided to video the next few Intensive Interaction sessions and sit down together to analyse what was going on. It wasn't entirely clear from the video but they got the hunch that Malcolm wasn't ready to end when the staff ended - that he was still emotionally and intellectually aroused - left with energy he didn't know what to do with.

The team decided to work more on the endings. They experimented with a more protracted close. They would stop imitating his movements but still comment on them for a while before gradually becoming quiet and just sitting with him for a while before moving on. They were fortunate to have found a solution with this and the furniture throwing stopped and the interactions developed new levels of complexity. If this had not have worked they were prepared for more discussion and teamwork but not to give up.

Josie

We were asked by a group of care staff to advise on a young woman, Josie, with whom they were just starting out with Intensive Interaction. Their problem was that Josie responded well for about 20 seconds and then suddenly hit out. We observed and tried this for ourselves and painfully found it to be true. Unusually we could not identify a signal that her mood was changing and pre-empt it that way. It seemed that although she enjoyed the interaction suddenly she could no longer cope and her tolerance and communication abilities were yet to be extended. We advised that they stop before twenty seconds and work instead on building her confidence with plenty of shorter 10-15 second episodes. Josie is coping well with these and becoming more smiley and trusting. We are urging the team not to rush to test out her threshold, but to let longer interactions come naturally.

Marcia

Marcia is deaf-blind and her interactive games with her mum involve a warm hug and during the embrace they exchange rhythmic pats on each other's back. While Marcia accepts her mum moving away at the end of the game without protest, her mum worries that the ending may be too abrupt when Marcia cannot see or hear her nearby. Without conscious planning Marcia's mum introduces a signalling system of both her hands squeezing Marcia's to say 'I'm finishing soon', and a one-handed squeeze to say 'I'm going now'. She doesn't see any observable change in Marcia with this system, but feels that it is working for them.

TROUBLESHOOTING

What about if the person always wants a game?

Being playful involves creating a different kind of atmosphere in which there is not the feeling of you, the carer or staff member, being in control or dominant. This is essential for realising the benefits of Intensive Interaction and interactive games we have talked about. We may often have a fear, however, that by relinquishing this feeling of control, we won't be able to establish it again if and when we need it. This is an important and complex issue. Playing interactive games together breaks down the barriers between us. It can also break down any fear of us felt by the person with learning difficulties. If the person at another time then becomes more difficult or challenging we may feel the need to assert ourselves and our control of the situation once again. It seems to us that it is vital here to be clear about what the issues really are.

Does control of the person/situation rely on an element of fear of us? If this is so, is this something we do, or should, want to recapture? Does the person need firm and consistent handling when their behaviour gets more extreme? If this is so, why does the game-playing interfere with this? Our involvement in Intensive Interaction should mean that we have got to know the person better and built some kind of relationship with them. This should help us, not undermine us, when boundaries need to be established. Part of the art of all this is in clear, meaningful communication. We need to become skilled in signalling - "this is game, this is fun" and "this is not acceptable, I am going to help you to behave in a different way".

What about when we don't feel playful?

Spending much of your day engaged in interactive game is a nice way of working with people with SLD. It is certainly more fulfilling that going through the motions of teaching or caring, and less stressful than having endless battles of will about behaviours. There are times, though, when you don't feel playful, that engaging in interactive game seems like the hardest work of all. We would not advise forcing yourself when this is the case. You won't be able to offer what the person with SLD needs from you and you may undo some of the progress you have achieved. You don't necessarily have to write off the whole day though. It may be that you need time to relax and get over your journey to work. You may need a little time to yourself after your child has given you a sleepless night. Look out for signs that you may be ready to play as well as signs that the person with SLD is ready to play. Allow yourself to be warmed up by them or by others having good sessions around you. If you are feeling low about how things are going during Intensive Interaction sessions it can be helpful to watch video footage to remind yourself what it's all about.

How does all this play fit in with achieving other targets?

While it is important to recognise the play qualities of interactive games, you should not think of this as time out from the real work of achieving real targets. The interactive games are likely to be the most intensive 'work' you do. It is during periods of engagement in meaningful interactions that the person with SLD is likely to be learning most and doing the most important activity for their development. You may feel you want to set targets for what you want the person with SLD to achieve in the coming months. Even if you don't formalise these, you will certainly have aims and hopes. It is helpful to have an idea about where you are going and what your priorities are. It is not helpful, however, to set targets for each session or day. This closes down your flexibility as an interactor and prevents you from being truly responsive. It means you will go into the activity of interacting with an agenda and too narrow a sense of task. If interactive games are to do what they do best in fostering development, they have to be game-led, child- (or adult-) led, and mutually enjoyable.

How do I know when an interactive game isn't appropriate any more?

We have stressed the importance of the earliest interactive games for establishing the learning needed at this stage and for later progress. For some staff working with people with SLD, Intensive Interaction is accepted as a necessity when there are few other options available because of the severity of the person's difficulties or isolation. Once they have accessed the person, and established a repertoire of games with good mutual involvement, they revert to a different interactive style. It is particularly tempting to do this when the staff are teachers under pressure to get results, or when you are working with adults whom we want to be performing at a more advanced level, or even when you are parents wanting so much for your child to develop. This can mean a jump from facilitating interactive play to directing learning.

What is more appropriate, however, is facilitating more sophisticated interactive games, with less support, and in different situations. We think it is more helpful to be on the look out for what to extend and develop, and how, rather than what to stop and when. The next chapter discusses this more fully.

SUMMARY

- What happens in Intensive Interaction sessions can be thought of as interactive games.

- Games have important qualities including joint activity, mutual involvement, repetition, turn-taking, intrinsic motivation, and opportunities for stress-free problem-solving.

- Effective games are stimulating, they come from responding and they involve rhythm, anticipation, repetition, and turn-taking.

- You may need to think through how to prepare, initiate and end interactive games.

- Interactive games are not time out from real work; they are the most intensive developmental activity you can do.

Chapter 5

KEEPING GOING AND GOING FURTHER

Sections in this chapter:

KEEPING GOING

MOVING ON FROM RESPONDING

We have suggested in Chapter Three that responsiveness is a key part of Intensive Interaction. Being responsive is about getting into a routine where responding comes naturally - where, for example, if your communication partner makes a sound you don't think twice about repeating it back to them or commenting "That's a good sound you're making". What is important is that you respond. This gives the communication partner the message that your sounds/movements/facial expressions have meaning - they are interesting to me - you are of value to me. This is vital in the early stages, but should we keep this up for ever?

If we want the people we work with, or care for, to become more able in their communications then we have to give some thought to our responding. For their communications and interactions to develop we may need to change how we communicate and interact - how we respond.

Responsiveness is a vital part of even the most sophisticated kinds of communication. We need to nod, look, agree, ask questions to be an effective communicator. Responsiveness, then, does not go away as the interactions and communications become more conventional. We don't need to replace responding with something else, but we do need to:

1. Adjust the way in which we respond, so that the communication becomes more sophisticated and conventional.

2. Adjust what we respond to, so that we can help our communication partner to move on.

Let us deal with the second point first. In the early stages of Intensive Interaction we are not likely to be too selective about what we respond to. We will rule out what we are not comfortable with - we won't imitate or celebrate masturbation or self-injury for example! While we may rule some things out, we won't be waiting for the best behaviour to come along before we respond. We will be ready to imitate almost all sounds; we will be prepared to join in with rocking and swaying; we will be able to make even a burp into a game. This is how it is in parent-baby interaction in the earliest stages. We watch infants with intense interest and respond to a squirm, the screwing up of a face, the involuntary blowing of saliva into bubbles.

In parent-baby interaction, however, things move on quickly. Soon parents are, without conscious thought, looking for changes in behaviour and responding particularly to these. At this time they are also looking for responses to changes of stimulus - did she hear her bath being prepared? can she feel that breeze? did she try to focus on that new face? It is these responses that they then respond to more. Parents also look for changes in how their infants respond - intuitively choosing the newest or most advanced behaviours to respond to. In this way, responding to all sounds gradually becomes responding only to those sounds which most are most like words. (This is a bit like 'shaping' in behavioural terms, but much more flexible and intuitive.)

As Intensive Interaction is based on parental interaction style we need to make these adjustments too. After we have established that you can have an effect, we help the person with SLD to move on by establishing you can have most effect by... This encourages them to experiment with their sounds and gestures. It encourages them to move from very individual (and limited) ways of behaving, to behaving in ways that more people are likely to understand and feel able to respond to.

These changes in responding might be intuitive for us - we are likely to want to celebrate a behaviour which is new for an individual, or a movement which is nearer to a gesture or a point, for example. As we have said before, however, this might take a bit more thinking and teamwork when the people we are communicating with have SLD and are more complex.   Without teamwork it may be that one person in the team is consciously selecting certain movements and treating them as gestures, that one person is doing this subconsciously, and that another is still responding to all movements. What is important in the beginning is that we respond. What is important for moving on is that we respond to the most advanced social and communication behaviours. The section on recognising progress later in this chapter gives pointers on what these are.

MOVING ON IN HOW WE RESPOND

As well as making changes in what we respond to, we also need to make changes in how we respond. This is all part of using Intensive Interaction to help our communication partners to move on.

There are all sorts of ways in which we can respond. Some responses fit better with some behaviours. Rocking and humming, for example, seem to elicit 'joining in' responses. These are things we can do together - at the same time - as part of building rapport. Other less continuous behaviours, such as occasional sounds, seem to prompt us to imitate - to copy what the other person has just done. When someone is involved in self-stimulating rituals our response can be a mixture of joining in and imitating.

These responses are great for getting to know the person better; for showing them that we are willing to join them on their terms; for building up tolerance of time spent in close proximity. In terms of communication development, though, we need to make changes to how we respond, as other responses have greater potential for helping the person, and the interaction, to move on.

One of the key ways in which we need to move on in our responses involves timing - shifting from joining in (being 'synchronous') to creating 'turn-taking'. Babies and parents move on from 'mutual gaze' to 'gaze coupling', that is from periods of looking at each other to taking turns in looking. They move on from babbling together, to dialogues where each takes a turn and where there are pauses and interruptions. These are a good rehearsal for real conversation later. In our interactions with individuals with SLD these things may be harder to achieve, and they certainly shouldn't be rushed, but we do need to be aware of how we might move on.

Another key part of moving on involves how we respond verbally to our communication partners - how and when we talk to them. With adults with SLD in particular we are under all sorts of pressure to use an adult-to-adult style of talk, but in Intensive Interaction this isn't very interesting or helpful. This tension between age-appropriate and developmentally appropriate speech, combined with a tendency to just join in or imitate, means that we may drop speech altogether in Intensive Interaction. This may help the flow of interaction in the early stages, but we do need to move on to bring verbal responses into the interactions and to adjust the way we talk as the person develops.

MOVING ON IN OUR INTERPRETATIONS

In earlier chapters we have talked about the importance of parents interpreting babies' behaviours as more advanced, social and meaningful than they really are. In Intensive Interaction therefore, we may treat a head movement as a 'hello' and a grunt as a 'go away'. The person with SLD may not consciously mean anything by their body language and vocalisations but we give them meaning as part of helping them to develop. This is another area where changes need to happen over time. The diagram below shows the stages we go through as we move on in our interpretations.

stage	type of interpretation	parent-baby example	Intensive Interaction example
level 1	interpret as social	baby: gurgles parent: smiles "yes, hello" baby: more gurgling parent: bigger smile "hello, hello, hello", presses nose into baby's tummy	Louis: slaps hand on chair three times, making loud, rhythmic noise Mel: replies with furniture slapping in the same rhythm, catches Louis's eye and smiles warmly
level 2	interpret as meaningful	baby: whimpers parent: makes soothing sounds, "you're tired aren't you little one" baby: begins to cry parent: picks baby up "yes, yes, you need a sleep"	Louis & Mel exchange 3 'turns' of furniture slapping. Mel, distracted, turns away, Louis, slaps chair loudly. Mel: "oh sorry, we haven't finished our game have we..." and joins in again.
level 3	interpret as intentional (action)	baby: yawns parent: interprets this as wanting a variation and changes activity. With rising, playful intonation she asks "oh, you're fed up with that are you? are you telling me you're fed up? are you?"	Louis is humming to himself while rocking on his chair. Mel, nearby is picking up on any pauses and inserting a sing-song response. Louis leaves a longer pause, Mel sees this as asking for more and sings more playfully as she approaches.
level 4	interpret as intentional (finding out)	baby: looks over mum's shoulder parent: follows baby's gaze and asks "what's over there eh? what are you looking at over there?"	Louis has been adding lots of variations into their imitation sing-song game. Mel sees this as finding out how flexible she can be and comments on this "you want to see if I can go that high do you?"

MOVING ON TO THE WIDER ENVIRONMENT

Another way in which interactions move on concerns their focus. In the early days (and possibly weeks and months with individuals with SLD) the focus of the interactions is just the two people involved in them. The focus is likely to be entirely on their sounds, or facial expressions or movements. This is great for establishing attention, interest and concentration. It is great for building relationship and trust. When these are well established, though, you will want to move on to more. Parents and babies increasingly move their focus to the wider world. We need to enable this to happen in Intensive Interaction too. To do this you have two main options.

- Follow the person's gaze and make what they are looking at the focus of your interaction.

  Examples might be chatting about the other person in the room who is being loud, playfully imitating some of that other person's sounds, asking questions about who might come through the door next, following the person as they wander - exploring with them.

- Introduce objects - play things other than yourself. At first you may need to bring them alive using playful sound effects etc, but eventually the two of you need to be focused together on the object rather than each other.

Focusing outwards forms the basis for joint attention. This will be needed later for having conversations, as you will need something to converse about, as and when the person moves on further still.

GENERALISATION

One of the criticisms of other approaches is that the person with SLD is often unable to transfer newly acquired skills to new situations, that is, to generalise. This has been a particular problem with behavioural approaches where the behaviour and the rewards are in danger of becoming associated with a particular place, or piece of equipment, or person. Intensive Interaction is concerned with much more meaningful learning and as such you should not be faced with generalisation as a problem in this way. Nonetheless, it is important that as communication partners you don't get stuck in a rut, having the same old conversation over and over again!

MOVING ON TO NEW GAMES

There is, then, a careful balance to be achieved between rehearsing the familiar routines and introducing new ones. This is often easily achieved by looking for slight variations in the response of the person with SLD that you can celebrate, and by introducing new variations yourself. You don't have to rush into new games, but you do need to be aware of opportunities where they arise. It can be helpful to keep a note of the kinds of interaction sequences the person with SLD has in their repertoire. You can then see them snowball - or not - in which case you can approach this problem as a team.

It is worth remembering that the very familiar interaction routines can provide a safe 'place' to return to at times of change, stress or distress. In contrast, the new games can be territory to be explored when the two of you are feeling good and interacting at your best.

MOVING ON TO NEW SETTINGS

It is also important for moving on that the interactions can take place in different settings. If the person with SLD has a preferred corner of a room, then it can be significant progress for them to move towards the centre of the room. If you have really positive interactions when the person with SLD is most relaxed in the swimming pool or bath, then you will want to (in time) extend this to other settings. A real bonus with this approach is that it does not require any special equipment or place and you will want to make the most of this flexibility. We do, after all, need to be able to communicate and relate to others wherever we are.

MOVING ON TO NEW PEOPLE

In the context of parenting the interactions mostly happen with the parent(s) and other caregivers. Babies though, also tend to trigger the interactive style they need and can understand from anyone who is around, including passers-by who just stop to say hello. All this adds up to healthy social development.

With individuals with SLD things may be different. We may be using the interactive style in an educational, occupational, or home support context rather than a parenting context. More people are likely to have frequent contact with the person who is less likely to be successful at getting their social and communication needs met. This means Intensive Interaction needs more planning as a shared endeavour. In the early stages just one communication partner may experience successful interactions, but eventually the person with SLD needs to be able to communicate with lots of different people. Introducing new people may happen naturally or may need to be planned for. Even with everyone using a common approach, different individuals have different styles and communication, by its very nature, needs to be flexible and responsive to these differences.

RECOGNISING PROGRESS

In Intensive Interaction success breeds success. Enjoying interactions means you interact more, which in turn means you (both the person with SLD and their communication partner) get better at interacting, which means interactions are even more enjoyable and so on. This means progress can happen without you really noticing it. In less ideal circumstances, however, it can feel like you've been interacting in the same ways, playing the same game, or having the same conversation, for ever. In these circumstances it can help you to keep going if you are able to recognise progress - to know what you are looking for as an indication that things are moving on.

LOOKING OUT FOR LONGER INTERACTIONS

One measure of progress is the length of time the interaction lasts. In the early stages a few seconds of togetherness is success. As time goes by the person with SLD should be able to sustain longer periods of attention and you should be able to hold that attention for longer. There will always be pauses, but the periods of joint attention should get longer.

LOOKING FOR OUT GREATER INVOLVEMENT

Another measure of progress is the amount of involvement the person with SLD can cope with. To start with they may rather passively watch your antics as you attempt to catch their interest. Perhaps even reaching this stage will be progress, although gradually they may look more, respond with changes of posture, slowing of rhythmic rocking or teeth-grinding, even becoming still. Responding with smiles and vocalisations linked to your behaviours are real signs of progress. Progress toward greater involvement may follow a fairly conventional pattern or may be much more idiosyncratic - particular to that individual. The art is to recognise what involvement looks like for that person.

Eve

Eve is seventeen and deaf-blind. She is very isolated and spends much of her time curled up in the foetal position. Ali has been working with her for a year, but finds it very hard to judge whether Eve is responding. When there is a movement or change of facial expression Ali doesn't know if it is a response to her as a person, a response to a physical sensation, or coincidental. She decides to hold back more with her stimulus - usually she strokes her hands and blows on them. When she places her hands around Eve's and waits, Eve gently prods her fingernail under Ali's. Ali imitates this gently and waits. Soon Eve reaches out with her finger nail again. After a few turns of this Ali knows that she and Eve have turned a corner - it may not be very conventional, but it is progress in their communication.

Tom is five and attends an assessment unit for pupils with autism. He looks very appealing and can often be seen sitting looking at a picture book or watching the fish in the fish tank. He is, however, extremely resistant to co-operating with others and generally uninterested in those around him. Eye contact has not been possible with Tom. Mary has worked with him for a year and has over the last couple of months started Intensive Interaction with him. She has found some rough and tumble games he likes and can hold his attention by playfully hiding his favourite toy behind her back and making it dramatically reappear. She was feeling that eye contact would never happen, when one day they played a hide the toy game with each of them at either end of the fish tank. Mary looked through the water at Tom - and found him looking back. He was sharing eye contact, through the safety barrier of the glass, and this was significant progress - for him.

Looking out for greater involvement may involve looking for new interactive behaviours such as looking and smiling. It should also, however, involve looking for better quality of involvement. Attending is an obvious important early stage. Anticipating is a higher order level of involvement - where the person with SLD shows awareness that their communication partner will take a turn or make a silly sound, for example. At their most involved the person will be 'engaged' in the interaction, that is, giving full attention, enjoying and anticipating and reciprocating. It is easier to feel that someone is engaged than to show it or describe it. You will know when it happens by how mutually satisfying the interaction feels.

LOOKING OUT FOR VARIATION

Interactions only accumulate and build in to more advanced social and communication abilities if we encourage and recognise variations. These variations, like signals of greater involvement, may well be idiosyncratic. As we have argued in terms of responding, it is important at first that we celebrate everything - all variations that we are comfortable with. We want to give the person with SLD the message that it is okay to explore - to experiment with new behaviour. There may, in time, be particular kinds of variation, such as new sounds or gesture-like movements, that we particularly value. It is important to recognise that by varying their interpersonal behaviours, the person with SLD shows us they feel secure to try out new things and that they are moving on.

LOOKING OUT FOR INITIATION

Other approaches have been successful at teaching people with SLD new social and communication skills. They have often, however, relied on the communication partner, or an artificial cue, to prompt this new skill into action. Often in the past we have given the person the skill - but not the motivation, the desire to - interact and communicate. Intensive Interaction

Eventually Michael becomes truly effective at initiating interactions.

is different because it places such a premium on pleasurable interaction. This helps with motivation. It also has the advantage of helping the communication partner to be very skilled and flexible with responding. This means that potential initiations do not go unnoticed. We ultimately want people who have found the social world difficult, to find it manageable and enjoyable, and to begin an interaction or 'conversation'.

It is important then to look for behaviours that can be interpreted as social acts - as conversation openers. It is also important to recognise when these really become so - become intentional initiations. All signs of wanting to be with others, and knowing how to initiate interactions, are major indications of progress and major incentives for us to keep going.

LOOKING OUT FOR INCREASED PARTICIPATION

As well as recognising the progress that happens within interactions, it is important for our feelings of effectiveness, to recognise other areas of progress too. We outlined what some of these might be in Chapter One.

Learning to communicate needs, relate to others and enjoy others' company, is bound to have a beneficial 'knock-on effect'. It is likely that the person with SLD will become less challenging and more willing to participate in activities generally. We may need to recognise that the reason for some of this progress lies within us, for example, it may be related to our being more tolerant, relaxed, or skilled. It is likely, though, that the person with SLD is more confident, trusting and skilled also. The truth is that developments do not happen in a vacuum; our development interacts with the development of those around us; social development interacts with development in other areas. This may be messier than we would like, but it is the nature of learning in naturalistic contexts.

Further Reading
Chapter 5 in *Interaction in Action: reflections on the use of Intensive Interaction* (Hewett & Nind, 1998) has a useful section on progress which describes the different kinds of progress to look for.

GOING FURTHER

GOING FURTHER TOWARDS OTHER APPROACHES

Intensive Interaction is clearly a good way to get people with SLD (and a range of additional difficulties) interested in other people and on the first steps towards social and communication competence. But for how long do we need to go on with Intensive Interaction and does a time come when this approach is no longer appropriate?

There is no clearly definable exit point for Intensive Interaction. We cannot say that once a person can do x they can go on to y approach. We would, however, refer you to the descriptions in Chapters One and Two of people for whom Intensive Interaction is meant. The person you interact with may fit one of these descriptions at the start, but become less like this as time goes on. In this situation the place of Intensive Interaction alongside other approaches, is likely to change as the person progresses. The way you 'do' Intensive Interaction may also change.

When someone cannot share space with other human beings, when they become upset at their closeness and perhaps even physically aggressive to themselves or others, there seems little point in having a broad approach or range of approaches and goals. In this instance we need to begin at the beginning. This beginning, we would argue, is not modifying their behaviour, but establishing relationships and the fundamentals of social communication. At this point, Intensive Interaction should be central - the primary way of going about the helping the person.

> **Meeting new challenges can be achieved painlessly by:**
>
> 1. Retaining time each day for interactive game - so we can remember how much fun we have together.
>
> 2. Bringing in new activities but going about them the old way - using the principles of Intensive Interaction to make them meaningful and enjoyable.
>
> 3. Bringing in approaches that complement Intensive Interaction such as incidental teaching, delay procedures, movement therapy (see additional reading).
>
> 4. Similarly avoiding approaches that clash with Intensive Interaction - that have a very different 'feel' and set of 'rules' (such as Walden, behaviour modification - see additional reading).

As the person becomes more amenable we will have the option of involving them in other activities. They will be able to participate, rather than comply, and we will need to make judgements about what could usefully be added to the person's routine, day care or education. As their communication abilities develop we have the option of using more formal approaches to teaching early language and so on.

The broadening of approaches should not feel too strange to someone with

SLD who has become comfortable with you and learnt to trust you. There will inevitably be problems if someone who has come to enjoy unconditional positive regard suddenly has to earn your approval. Similarly, it would not be helpful for you to make a sudden jump from a nurturing interactive style to being more directive and demanding. Part of going further is having new experiences and meeting new challenges, but this transition needs to be as seamless as possible - to feel right for all concerned. Some approaches and activities would seem to 'grow out of' Intensive Interaction and others would seem to conflict on a level of ethos and practice.

GOING FURTHER TOWARDS SPEECH OR SIGN

Some people with SLD you 'do' Intensive Interaction with will naturally seem to be progressing towards the development of speech or sign, that is, towards using symbolic communication. You can help them towards this by pushing the boundaries of what you do with Intensive Interaction. This will involve the continuing use of the principles together with your intuitions. As well as this you will need to add in some reflection on what kind of support beginning speech/sign users need.

Various developments may make you aware that the person you are working with is moving towards speech. For example, they may increasingly be using various vocalisations; the range of those vocalisations may seem to be growing quickly; some of their vocalisations may sound increasingly word-like; you may find yourself intuitively using more speech as commentary during the interactions; or the person with SLD may be using more gesture, particularly finger pointing or head pointing. Another compelling sign may be that you regularly have successful interactions, perhaps lasting ten or more minutes, where the person with SLD shows a great deal of interest and concentration. You may then begin to wonder about the next development.

The development of speech or signing will need the person with SLD to really be able to attend to you and show it. Think about what stage of development a baby is at by the time they move on to language use. By then, they are truly sophisticated communicators who love to be social and who practise their communication and social abilities almost constantly. This comparison with normal patterns of development can be helpful in reassuring you about how much preparation is needed before speech begins.

It is worth mentioning however, that some people with SLD, particularly those who also have autistic spectrum disorders, can develop in different ways. They may develop use of speech without some of the basic abilities to interact that we have discussed here. Such individuals will still need to learn these interpersonal skills after they have learned to talk, and Intensive Interaction activities can help them to develop. If interpersonal skills are a major area of difficulty for a verbal individual, however, you will need even more, not less, sensitive and skilled application of the principles and techniques.

Going further towards speech and sign may just mean doing more of the same - rehearsing for later symbolic communication. It may also mean that you look for the gaps in the foundations of communication and working on, or rather 'playing' with, those (see box below). This makes the interactive activity more deliberately purposeful. The art then is to be purposeful without making it feel like a task.

Possible gaps in the foundations for language and ways of working on them:

'Object permanence' - know that things still exist when we can no longer see them. This is the foundation for later symbol use. Lots of interactive games help with this.

Commentary:
'where's it gone.... ooh! here it is'

peek-a-boo

Imitation - the ability to imitate gesture, vocalisations, intonation, strings of syllables etc

"murm, murm"
"You're very chatty today, aren't you? murm, murm, murm, murm" (faster rhythm)
"mum, murm, murm" (same rhythm)

Know about cause and effect - know that if I do this I can make this happen. Many of our interactions will already have operated around the principle of responsiveness, resulting in the person having a sense of their own agency - their ability to cause an affect in us.

Commentary:
Jon gives a sideways glance at Kath - Kath looks out of the corner of her eye too and winks. on quickly looks away, but a few seconds later tries again and gets the same result. After the third and fourth try they are both aware of the game and share a smile.

Communicative intention - the desire or need to communicate. All of the interactions where we interpret some communication intent set the scene for this. All our responding to the slightest signal will have helped to develop awareness of the potential to communicate. We can also deliberately set up games which involve the need to communicate.

Commentary:
Sarah bounces her son on her knee, singing a rhyme, she pauses at a key moment in the routine and wide-eyed waits for some sign that he wants more. He gives a slight jerk of his body and she instantly laughs and dramatically resumes the bouncing and rhyme.

Capable of jointly attending to objects, events and people - having something to have a conversation about. Again the basis of this is attending to each other and this moves on to a broadening of focus discussed earlier in this chapter.

Commentary:
Jon repeatedly spins a beaker on the floor. His mum copies with a beaker of her own. Jon occasionally glances over. His dad then joins in and produces a much bigger beaker that makes a different sound. As he spins they all watch intently.

Further Reading

Coupe O'Kane & Goldbart (1998) *Communication Before Speech: Development and Assessment.* London: David Fulton.

Beveridge, Conti-Ramsden & Leudar (1989) *Language and Communication in People with Learning Disabilities.* London: Routledge.

For speech/sign to develop, the person with SLD also needs you to provide a helpful style of talking or signing yourself. We have already talked in this book about the verbal style that parents use (motherese) to introduce the baby to language in a way that matches their developmental level and needs. In Intensive Interaction this verbal style (summarised in the box on the right) is often readily adopted, especially if the person with SLD is still a child and there are fewer tensions with 'age-appropriateness' concepts.

> **A helpful style of talking involves:**
>
> • slower speech
>
> • speech that is high-pitched or varying in pitch
>
> • simple vocabulary
>
> • simple grammar
>
> • lots of repetition
>
> • talking about the here and now
>
> • lots of questions
>
> • an expectation of a reply
>
> • few commands

It is also quite possible that your Intensive Interaction sessions, so far, have had no verbal content - that you engage the person through non-verbal means. This is more likely to be the case when you are imitating vocalisations leaving little room for speech, or when you feel (perhaps intuitively) that speech would get in the way of your mutual enjoyment. This is fine for the early stages when the best communications may be those that are at a basic, idiosyncratic level.

To help the person with SLD to go further towards speech/sign, the time will come when they need you to offer a running commentary to highlight your joint attention. They will probably need you to adapt your language to focus on what is happening, here and now, in simple terms. Using a rhythmic, melodic style with lots of questions and few directives will help to make your speech (or sign) interesting. You will need to enable the person to develop their first meanings, that is, their single words or approximations or gestures which are used to communicate something. Again, you can be deliberately purposeful in your choice of interactions to support this process. By remembering the kinds of communications that typically emerge early in this process with babies, you can be more aware of opportunities where they arise. The box below gives a brief summary of some of the categories and suggestions for activities in this process.

Existence - naming an interesting object	It may be that first naming is of the thing the person with SLD twiddles or spins - the focus of their preoccupation.
Disappearance - commenting on an object vanishing or not being where it's supposed to be	'gone' This first word emerges quite naturally in 'where's it gone?' and peek-a-boo type games.
Recurrence - wanting something to happen again	'again', 'more' Again, the need for this first word comes naturally in games that are great fun and that involve a pregnant pause before the next burst.
Action - wanting something to happen	'go', 'up' Skillful use of build-up and anticipation in e.g. 'ready, steady... GO!' and '1,2,3 ... UP!' may prepare the ground for this kind of first word to emerge.

At this stage the interactions may have more 'specialised' activities within them. You may need to become especially attentive to the encouragement of vocalisations, particularly responding to vocalisations which sound like a word by using that word yourself in a pleasurable response. You might reduce the other things you do in response to focus on these vocal responses, if only for part of the interaction. If the person you are working with is not naturally developing a pointing gesture, you might start introducing your own point gesture at a new 'object' within the interactions.

Starting to point together and focus on what is being pointed at is really useful in speech rehearsal - it promotes pointing/labelling games. Pointing together is a good and pleasurable game. It enables you to make a speech response, naming the thing being pointed at, but it also enables you to introduce other words which are directly relevant - "what? where? who? which?". This can add further enjoyable dimensions to the speech game, like teasing by pretending not to recognise the thing being pointed at. You will want to establish enjoyable repetitions of the pointing/labelling games, with the words being rehearsed over and over again. Pointing games are also a very direct method of increasingly bringing aspects of the world around you within the interaction, naming them and making them part of what is taking place between you.

Of course, the expectation here is that the person with SLD will have developed sufficiently to be interested by what is taking place, and have the motivation to increasingly imitate what you are saying. With developing infants, this is such a natural and quick process that we hardly notice what it is that we do to make it happen. For a person with SLD however, it will take longer, may need more repetitions, we may need to be more deliberate, and there may be a limit to the amount of speech the person can learn.

There are other communication functions that may emerge too, and also form the basis for game activities. Examples might be use of possession words such as 'mine', rejection words 'no' , acceptance words 'yes, yeah' and 'agent' - 'me' (I want to...). In the early stages of the person developing use of some speech, it is a good idea to keep track of the words they are successfully using and to monitor further progress. This will help you to feel rewarded and effective as a communication partner or teacher who is clearly making progress, and this should further motivate you.

It makes sense that the emergence of language is a possible outcome of Intensive Interaction. However, for many people with SLD this will not happen. We would not want you to see this as a failure. Intensive Interaction provides a way of enhancing the quality of someone's life while also preparing them with good foundations for ongoing development. Development of basic social and communication abilities can result in a fundamental change in the quality of life for an individual with SLD (and those around them) and this achievement in itself should be celebrated.

SUMMARY

- Intensive Interaction is a useful approach for introducing people with SLD to the pleasures of social interaction. It is good for establishing the fundamentals of social and communication development.

- It is possible to keep going with Intensive Interaction once these basics are established.

- To keep going you need to ensure that the interactions broaden out and become more advanced.

- This involves responding to, and with, more sophisticated interactive behaviours.

- This also involves moving on to new games, settings and people.

- To continue to feel, and be, effective you need to recognise the progress you are making as communication partners.

- This involves looking out for longer interactions, greater involvement, new variations, initiation of social contact and increased participation in activities generally.

- By keeping going you may be able to introduce new, compatible approaches and move the person with SLD further towards speech or sign language.

Chapter 6

WORKPLACE ISSUES

Sections in this chapter:

THE ISSUES

The purpose of this book is to give practical guidance on Intensive Interaction. The bulk of this guidance has focused on the actual practice of the approach. There are other practical issues associated with the approach, however, that we explore in this chapter. These issues arise from using Intensive Interaction in the workplace where there are complications which do not arise for parents. As parents (or other close caregivers) at home, no one expects you not to touch or get attached to the person with SLD. The appropriateness of what you do is not policed in same way and you are not so accountable for your actions. In contrast, Intensive Interaction in the workplace raises these issues, and also practical matters of teamwork and operating within sensible safeguards for you and the people with SLD who use your service.

This chapter, then, is much more relevant for staff, be they teachers, care assistants, home or day support staff and their managers, speech or occupational therapists or whatever. If you are a parent using this book you won't find direct relevance for you here, but you may be able to apply some of the ideas. You may also find the chapter of interest in terms of the kinds of guidelines day centres, residential homes etc may operate.

TEAMWORK

PULLING TOGETHER

One of the major advantages to a group home, day centre, college or school, as a context for Intensive Interaction is the teamwork opportunities this offers. In the family context interactions may become stale or tense or unrewarding because there are fewer opportunities to share observations and feelings about interactions with others. With a range of communication partners you can share problems and successes and think through together strategies for accessing someone who is particularly remote or moving someone on who has 'got stuck'. You are also less likely to leave the person with SLD bereft or disorientated when staff move on as they inevitably do.

The team situation is not so ideal, however, if there is not a shared ethos but rather a range of views and approaches in operation. This can be confusing and result in none of the approaches being adopted fully. We really do recommend that if you are using Intensive Interaction in your workplace that some energy is put into developing a situation where everyone pulls together. This is important whatever your approach, but because Intensive Interaction requires you to use your personality and interpersonal skills it is particularly

important that you feel comfortable with your colleagues. If you are feeling embarrassed or awkward interacting in front of colleagues you may be pushed into interacting in 'private'. This can put you and the person with SLD into a vulnerable position (see later sections in this chapter). Another consequence of colleagues not pulling together is missed opportunities to learn from each other and to intensify your collective interactive efforts to make an impact on the most challenging of students/service users.

Pulling together can operate at a number of levels. From our experience it is worth spending time on the kinds of activities listed below.

- Talking to each other about who Intensive Interaction might be appropriate for and why.

- Talking through the controversial issues of age-appropriateness, use of physical contact etc and coming to some shared position everyone can live with.

- Drawing up policies and safeguards together.

- Observing each other, even video recording each other and exchanging feedback. There needs to be a good supportive framework for doing this which ensures that criticism is constructive and vulnerability respected.

- Covering aspects of each other's work to make time for observation and one-to-one sessions.

- Having problem-solving sessions to talk through possible strategies for someone where interaction is particularly challenging.

- Participating in staff training together.

- Setting up situations where you jointly explain Intensive Interaction to parents, governors and other interested parties.

SUPPORT FROM THE TOP

Just as it is important that colleagues support each other, so it is also vital that managers understand what staff members are trying to achieve with Intensive Interaction. An uninformed manager could mistake careful observation for sitting around, or interactive play for being silly in a disrespectful way. This could leave the staff member vulnerable and curtail the experience for the person with SLD. Managers, team leaders, etc are accountable for what goes on in the workplace and so they need to understand and support the practice of Intensive Interaction.

Sometimes it is the managers who instigate Intensive Interaction. At other times it is one or two staff members who go it alone, or who attempt to disseminate their knowledge of Intensive Interaction to colleagues. However Intensive Interaction starts, the sooner there is full staff dialogue about it, and a shared ethos and shared practice the better. If you are trying Intensive Interaction out as a new approach for you, or for the first time with an individual with SLD, it may be worth getting the manager to sit in on some sessions to get a feel for the approach. It may also be worth getting them to have a go. Actually 'doing' Intensive Interaction can help to dispel some uneasiness that some people feel. Getting a free rein to explore Intensive Interaction feels great at first, but getting interested involvement from the top is better in the long term. This way you are more likely to get good teamwork, good safeguards and adequate staffing levels.

SHARING GOOD PRACTICE

Good teamwork and good management support are important for enabling the sharing of good practice to happen. You will also need an ethos which supports positive interactions as a team endeavour and does not focus on individual achievements. Different staff need to feel that they can use their unique interactive style, whilst still applying the Intensive Interaction principles. At the same time they should feel duty-bound to share with colleagues what they think, or feel, works for them.

In a group situation, Intensive Interaction is about developing relationships as part of developing social and communication abilities, rather than as part of an exclusive, permanent bond. Sharing good practice means that there can be turn-over of staff without too much disruption for the service-users. It means that the people with SLD who are involved get a rich and varied interactive experience and a consistently meaningful one. It means that when things get difficult or stressful, or when someone simply seems to be not moving on, there is much greater likelihood of finding a positive way forward.

Sharing good practice can happen in a number of ways.

NHS

A National Health Service Learning Disability Trust is adopting Intensive Interaction as an approach for people with profound learning disabilities throughout its home support and day services. The multi-disciplinary support team have all had training on the approach and are acting as catalysts and support workers. The team leaders all had training together. Next local clusters of residential staff participated in training. As they got going, a peer supervision system was set-up where those using the approach met monthly, with the occupational therapists and psychologists. At each meeting they share an individual 'case' or two, using video clips where possible, and discuss successes, problems and possible next moves.

Two teachers

Two teachers and their two assistants in a school for children with SLD are keeping daily records of their best interactions sessions with their pupils. Each week they take turns to go through all the record forms and pick out issues for discussion as a team. These might be new achievements, instances where a pupil is interacting well with one person in the team only, or similar problems reported by all the team.

FINDING TIME

Intensive Interaction obviously requires time for quality one-to-one attention. Finding or making this time can be a major challenge in the workplace. It is a challenge that cannot be met without good teamwork. You need to create situations in which you have no other role than to be available to one of the service-users for quality interaction. To do this you need to be sure that other colleagues are covering your other roles. Another way of finding time is to re-evaluate what your priorities are, so that not finding time is no longer an option!

You need to find time to be with people and available for interaction. This does not necessarily mean that the time when they are at their most relaxed and open for interaction will co-incide with the time that best suits you. On the whole, it is you who needs to be flexible here. Observation and trial and error will help you to find their good times. It is largely a 'can do' attitude that will enable you to fit in with these good times. It is important that you have some protected time for interaction sessions. There are no guarantees that you will have good interactions within these sessions, but it is more likely. You also need to be on the look out for other opportunities for interaction. These are the incidental interactions, as you pass each other in the hall, as you help someone to have a bath and so on. Sometimes you can be more relaxed if you don't feel the pressure to perform or get an interactive result!

In one house

In one house the team were all trying Intensive Interaction. They soon found that creating quality one-to-one time was a major hurdle. As soon as they approached a tenant or began an observation, the phone rang or the doorbell went. Inevitably several people stopped what they were doing to attend to this, and others had their concentration spoiled. After a team meeting they agreed to a rota for this role, ensuring that only one person responded to the phone and door, leaving others to focus on the interactions. This simple measure increased the time available and made sure it was better used.

In another house

In another house the staff said all their time was taken up with activities and domestic chores. Just spending 10 minutes sitting with a client felt lazy - not an option. The staff reviewed this and decided that they were not achieving quality of life for their clients. Some of the activities were shortened and the ethos changed.

TROUBLESHOOTING

The following problems are amongst those we, or the staff we have worked closely with, have faced and some of the ways forward which have helped.

What can you do about colleague(s) who won't join in?
- Give them time. For some people Intensive Interaction is very different from the ways they have worked in the past. This means that adopting the approach is a journey into the unknown. While for some this is an exciting challenge for others this is frightening which might mean they resist. Backing them into a corner and insisting that this is how it's done from now on won't help them to feel at ease with the development. Put

in this position they will probably undermine the approach, either consciously or unconsciously. Allowing them to see others using Intensive Interaction and letting them join in as and when they feel comfortable may be a better alternative.

- Try it out. You may be able to encourage them to try Intensive Interaction with a client for whom they have particular affection. It is likely that aspects of their interactive style with one individual resembles Intensive Interaction although they may not have thought about it in these terms.

- Organise a trial period. If the resistant colleague is outspoken in their objections to the approach you may need to make a pact along the lines of "let me try it for six weeks and if there's been no success we'll drop the matter completely". The colleague may see this as a route to an end of the matter, but invariably progress is made and they may be won over.

- Organise staffing according to strengths. Some staff will never be comfortable with Intensive Interaction and there is little point in making them. A relaxed approach and a willingness to enjoy the person with SLD on their own terms is essential. If this seems out of the question then perhaps that colleague has great strengths to offer with more able service-users. Be careful not to make assumptions about who these staff will be. Staff of all ages and varying levels of extrovert behaviour have all adopted Intensive Interaction readily.

- Enable the staff member to move on. This is a last resort for individuals who undermine the efforts of others. Staff who are unable to share any power with people with SLD, who like to be in control and who shout and use their physical presence may not make the adjustment in approach or allow others to do so either. Staff who do not like the people with SLD they work for will similarly not have a place in an Intensive Interaction environment.

What can you do when one set of staff use the approach more than another?
- Prioritise communication. Situations can arise in residential establishments where one shift is pulling together with Intensive Interaction and the other shift, although keen, is less able to practice the approach. Whether Intensive Interaction is in use or not, this is really a management issue, but Intensive Interaction can bring poor communication to the forefront. At some point time has to be found for communication to happen. This doesn't have to be new time or mean more resources, it just means different priorities and using the staffing time you do have in a different way. Sometimes managers 'getting their hands dirty' can free up time. Sometimes rotas can be re-organised to help with this.

- Peer supervision groups and joint training can be helpful for sharing ideas and spreading motivation.

- A strong steer from the top. Situations can arise in schools where Intensive Interaction is big in the nursery and upper primary, but less in evidence in lower primary and virtually non-existent on the secondary site. This can be a communication issue again. It can also be a problem related to where staff are located and moving some people around may be necessary. A whole school approach and a common philosophy is, however, the only real answer to achieving a coherent framework across an organisation.

ACCOUNTABILITY

WRITTEN POLICIES

In the workplace we are accountable; that is, we are responsible to others, and for our actions. We may be obliged to answer for what we do and we should be able to clearly explain the reasons for it. It is not always readily apparent to someone who is uninformed what on earth it is we are doing in Intensive Interaction! Our actions could be misinterpreted unless we are clear about the very sound basis for them.

Wherever you work there should be written policies. These may operate at

different levels of the organisation. For example a school may have a School Development Plan for the whole school, a Secondary Department Policy covering pupils of a certain age and a Personal, Social and Health Education policy covering a certain curriculum area. Similarly a group home may have a day care policy, an advocacy policy, a policy on intimate care and so on.

Having a policy for Intensive Interaction or having Intensive Interaction outlined in one or more of the other policies is useful for accountability. This protects everyone involved. Writing policies should not be seen as a defensive act, however. There is a lot to be gained from writing policies together in terms of teamwork, clarity and shared ethos.

There may be complete or partial overlap between a written policy and written safeguards which are covered in the next section. For us though, a policy should be a positive statement about adopting a stance or set of practices, the reasons for it, and what you hope to achieve.

Overlapping Policies

In some organisations the policy already in existence is clearly compatible with the introduction of Intensive Interaction. Chris Addis explains this in his chapter in Interaction in Action (Hewett & Nind, 1998, p.25) in which he outlines the objectives in place in his unit for pupils who have multi-sensory impairment:

"We strive to let the students know that they are welcomed and loved and respected and heard, and that they are fun to be with. We offer them as much opportunity as possible to express choice, and we use as many means as possible to elicit communication."

Filling Policy Gaps

In other organisations the introduction of an Intensive Interaction policy is about filling a gap in policy and practice. One SLD school was aware, following an OFSTED inspection report, that not enough was being done for pupils with profound and multiple learning difficulties in the area of communication. They chose to introduce an Intensive Interaction policy as a specific response to this. They saw this as strong both in words and practice and they could be clear about the basis for the approach in developmental psychology, what they hoped to achieve and how they were going about achieving it.

INDIVIDUAL RECORDS & PLANS

The policy is the written statement at some general level. There also needs to be written statements at the level of the individual. Our accountability is further enhanced if individual education or care plan states that Intensive Interaction has some part to play - either central or peripheral. We are accountable to our service-users too and if Intensive Interaction is written into person-centred planning tools, such as Essential Lifestyle Planning, for example, we are obliged to offer it. This can be helpful when it comes to selecting new staff and appointing colleagues sympathetic to the approach. Individual planning can make issues of link workers and the need for mentoring of new staff explicit.

It follows from having an individual plan that there needs to be individual records. Such records should establish a baseline (see Chapter Two) for that person and note the progress they make at key points (perhaps termly or annually) or when the new developments occur.

Individual records help with accountability in that they show that what you are doing (for the reasons you have specified) is having a positive affect. They are of course also helpful in informing you of what is happening or not happening at a practical level, so that you can review and improve your practice. This is a kind of accountability too - to yourself.

Some record sheets that you might want to use or adapt are included in the Appendices.

Further Reading

Many of the accounts of Intensive Interaction in *Interaction in Action* (Hewett & Nind, 1998) include example of how the practitioners recorded progress. Record-keeping is also discussed in *Access to Communication* (Nind & Hewett, 1994, pp154-159).

USE OF VIDEO

If you have access to a video camera, video recordings of your use of Intensive Interaction are invaluable. You and the people with SLD you work with may need to get used to the camera being around before you can gather useful footage of people behaving naturally. You will need to get agreement to film from parents of children, or from key supporters of adults not able to give informed consent due to the extent of their learning disabilities. This should make explicit what the video is for (progress records, training purposes, research etc). You will also need to make sure camera operators learn to use the equipment well - as silhouetted or fuzzy shapes and clips of people's feet are useless. With video working well for you though, you will enjoy the following benefits.

- The chance to review what it is that you do that is or is not working in the interactions.

- The chance to look again at the responses of the person with SLD, perhaps seeing something you missed at the time.

- The chance to compare interactions happening now with those you recorded six months ago (or with baseline video - prior to using the approach) - this can be very uplifting and useful for new staff who won't be aware of the changes made.

- The chance to share discussion of video to help with staff training and team-building.

- The opportunity to show to interested parties exactly what it is you do with Intensive Interaction (part of accountability).

TROUBLESHOOTING

Is it appropriate to 'do' Intensive Interaction in public places?

We are often challenged in training sessions by 'centreless day service' workers with the statement "our clients are out and about in the community all the time - we couldn't possibly do Intensive Interaction in public - they would look undignified". Our response to whether it's appropriate is yes, but...

- Only if you feel comfortable. The concern about public Intensive Interaction making the person with SLD look odd is often a disguised concern that we might look odd. This is quite understandable. No one wants to make a fool of themselves or have what they are doing misinterpreted. If you feel embarrassed about the interaction you are unlikely to engage the attention of the person with SLD and there is little point in trying. Using bits of the interactive style but in a suppressed, unsuccessful way will look peculiar to onlookers.

- Weigh up the situation. Are there really hoards of onlookers interested in you, or are other people in the park having a good time themselves - being relaxed and playful too. Why should the fun or emotional needs of a person with SLD be more strictly 'policed' than any one else?

- Choose your interactive game wisely. We concede that the queue in Tesco may not be the best place to have your liveliest, noisiest romp! However, we also argue that if the person is ready for an interaction session, it is not okay to act as if you don't know them... to respond with a cold or distant or controlling interactive style reserved for these situations. This is unfairly confusing for the person with SLD and will undermine your other achievements. If you have built up a repertoire of interactions then you should have lively ones and low key ones to call on. Guide the interaction towards the latter. This is a compromise between the person's entitlement and societal pressures.

What if I get challenged or criticised for 'doing' Intensive Interaction?

- Know what you're doing and why. Give yourself and colleagues plenty of time to discuss the approach, to read about it, and to be clear about its strong foundations and logic. Meeting people's needs is not something to be ashamed about!

- Have reading matter available. Depending on who is questioning you, it may be helpful to refer them to your policy, to an individual education or care plan, to one of the books on Intensive Interaction, or even to a published evaluation of its effectiveness. You are accountable and often people genuinely want to know what this (at first glance strange) interactive behaviour is all about

- Be confident. The more confident you are in what you do the less likely people are to question you. (This has often been proved in schools with OFSTED inspectors!)

Further Reading

Published evaluations and discussions of the effectiveness of Intensive Interaction are available. See:

Nind (1996) 'Efficacy of Intensive Interaction', European Journal of Special Needs Education, 11, 48-66 (technical - lots of data)

Watson & Fisher (1997) 'Evaluating the effectiveness of Intensive Interaction teaching with pupils with profound and complex learning difficulties', British Journal of Special Education, 24, 2, 80-87 (compared to an alternative approach)

Hewett & Nind (1998) *Interaction in Action* (David Fulton) (personal accounts including those of parents and health and social services staff)

Lovell, Jones & Ephraim (1998) 'The effect of Intensive Interaction on the sociability of a man with severe intellectual disabilities', International Journal of Practical Approaches to Disability, 23, 2/3, 3-9 (single case study)

Nind (1999) 'Intensive Interaction and autism: a useful approach?', British Journal of Special Education, 26, 2, 96-102 (weighs up the evidence)

SAFE PRACTICE GUIDELINES

WHY SAFE PRACTICE GUIDELINES?

We have talked about teamwork and accountability as workplace issues. They are, of course, important issues whatever the approach adopted by the organisation. The same is true of having safe practice guidelines. When we work with people who are vulnerable we need to have a set of rules or procedures that ensure their safety - these are what we mean by safe practice guidelines (or safeguards for short). Such safeguards also protect us as staff members too. We need to be sure that when we focus on interaction and relationship that we are not making people more vulnerable or more anxious.

Most practitioners involved with Intensive Interaction feel very comfortable about this, but writing safe practice guidelines ensures that we attend to detail and attempt to resolve the inevitable tensions in our work (to touch or not to touch; to play or not to play etc). The very process of drawing up the safeguards is an important one for working towards a shared ethos and set of practices. Even if we do not end up with a perfect document, we will have had the important discussions. Indeed we suggest that a set of guidelines is always a working document - always under review.

It is because we place value on the process of discussing and writing safe practice guidelines that we have resisted including them ready-prepared in this book. We will, however, highlight some of the areas you may want to cover.

AREAS TO SAFEGUARD

Physical contact

- You will need to decide whether this is 'permitted' and on what basis.

- For all pupils/service users?

- For all staff members? In what situations?

- How will you be confident that the touch is welcomed and appropriate?

Sexual Arousal

- You will need to decide how you will respond if sexual arousal becomes evident during an interaction.

- How will you know?

- How will you know if the interaction is connected?

- How will you ensure that the person with SLD gets the right message?

- What is the right message - is it that sex is not a problem, but not what the interactions are about?

- How will you ensure that the interactions still happen for someone who spends a lot of time masturbating?

- Do you need special rules for male staff?

- Have you remembered not to presume that everyone is heterosexual?

- Are you doing everything you can to protect the vulnerable from abuse and the staff members from improper allegations of abuse?

Consent to Interact

- You will need to decide who needs Intensive Interaction and what to do if they appear not to want it.

- How will you know if the person wants to join in?

- If they don't, do they know what it's like? Not interacting is unlikely to be an informed choice.

- Is it right to attempt Intensive Interaction with someone who seems to want to be left alone?

- If you are clear about your reasons for proceeding how can you be as gentle and respectful as possible?

When and Where
- Linked to earlier points you will need to decide if there are any no-go zones or situations for interaction.

- Is it okay for you and the person with SLD to be alone in the playroom for Intensive Interaction? In the bedroom? If the staff member is male? If the door is open? If it is in their programme and regularly recorded on video?

The questions we have posed above are difficult ones. Your first response may be that they are too difficult to resolve and so you will opt out from Intensive Interaction. We sympathise. We would, however, remind you that there is not a vast array of alternative approaches out there for people with this level of difficulty and:

1. whether you do Intensive Interaction or not many of these factors will still be an issue;

2. there are no right or wrong answers - just an honest attempt to do the best you can - with the option to change the guidelines at any time if they are not workable.

Newtown Road

The staff at 4 Newtown Road agreed that Intensive Interaction should not take place when there was just one staff member and one tenant alone in the tenant's bedroom. Unfortunately this turned out to be the place where Annie was most relaxed and most likely to give eye contact. It felt very artificial and awkward not to be playful here. Although sessions weren't programmed to happen in her room, lots of incidental opportunities were being missed. Her keyworker put forward a change of guidelines. It was then agreed that staff re-think 'bedrooms' as more versatile personal spaces where one-to-one interaction may happen - with the door open.

Honeyhill school had happily incorporated Intensive Interaction into the curriculum. The staff wrote guidelines for when and how often sessions should happen and how they should be recorded. They involved parents and kept them informed. A governor questioned whether there should be different rules for male staff, and these were devised with some care. There was only 1 male teacher and 1 male assistant and they felt singled out and uncomfortable. Other staff felt awkward around them too. The relaxed atmosphere needed for Intensive Interaction seemed to evaporate overnight and although things settled down a bit, this did not return.

The staff group reviewed the guidelines and the implications for them and in consultation with parents re-wrote them. Over the next few weeks they found the guidelines more workable, but agreed to review them again at the end of the year.

TROUBLESHOOTING

What if everyone is so different that general guidelines are hard to write?

Build this in. Safe practice guidelines need to take into account that people are of different ages and genders and have different abilities, disabilities and needs. You may need a general framework of safeguards followed by some specific points. For example, a general point that Intensive Interaction will mostly happen in the communal areas, may be followed by a specific reference to Kenny who interacts best in the Jacuzzi bath, and a note that this will be timetabled for when other staff are nearby. It may be that the guidelines have a 'normally' clause with exceptions to the 'rule' needing to be agreed by more than one member of the team. It may be that the guidelines simply list the scenarios when team discussions are needed. For example, a guideline may state that physical contact is an accepted mode of communication in the establishment, but this must be raised for staff discussion if a) the individual ever becomes distressed during physical interactions; b) the individual has a known history of abuse; or c) familiar staff from the regular team are absent. The complexities of the individual situations make the need for safeguards greater not lesser, but time will be needed to work through them.

SUMMARY

- Intensive Interaction is most effective when there is good teamwork that enables you to share successes and strategies and work through problems together.

- To get the most from Intensive Interaction support from management of an organisation or service is needed.

- A major organisational issue for Intensive Interaction is finding the time for quality one-to-one work.

- A shared ethos helps to embed Intensive Interaction in everyday practice.

- There is a need for written policies and safe practice guidelines; these should be developed as part of the teamwork and open to regular review and revision.

- Individual records and video evidence help to enhance your practice and educate others.

APPENDICES

Appendix 1
Record Form One (minimal prompts)

Appendix 2
Example of Completed Record Form One

Appendix 3
Record Form Two (detailed prompts)

Appendix 4
Example of Completed Record Form Two

Appendix 5
Self-appraisal Form for Interactive Style

References

APPENDIX ONE: RECORD FORM ONE   (MINIMAL PROMPTS)

INTERACTION DAILY RECORD

Interaction partners:

Date and time:

Place and situation:

What happened?   (describe the sequence)

What was significant?   (new, different, possibly progress)

How did it feel?   (my response and performance)

Other comments

APPENDIX TWO: EXAMPLE OF COMPLETED RECORD FORM ONE

INTERACTION DAILY RECORD

Interaction partners:

Date and time:

Place and situation:

What happened?   (describe the sequence)
Tom was wandering, distracted around room. I followed for a while then sat on the bean bag by the window where he passed often. He continued to move round the room - visited where I was often - and glanced at me on and off. Patted my knees each time to encourage him to flop down with me. Got longer glances. Patted floor beside me. Patted by my feet. Tom interested but didn't join me.

What was significant?   (new, different, possibly progress)
Definite interest on Tom's part. Quite a lot of looking. Possibly a hint of playfulness - was he teasing me but coming near but never sitting?

How did it feel?   (my response and performance)
Got better once I stopped following him and sat - good move - we both relaxed. Sparkle of interest was promising. Felt like we were testing each other out - I was determined to keep low-key and not pressure him. Still think although it didn't develop much further today that this was wise.

Other comments
Must try to set this up again.
Should I chat more - 'come and see me' ?

APPENDIX THREE: RECORD FORM TWO   (DETAILED PROMPTS)

INTERACTION DAILY RECORD

Interaction partners:

Date and time:

Place and situation:

1. Did your interaction partner enjoy the session and any parts of it in particular?

2. If not, when and why?

3. How effective was the signalling today?

4. Did anything new happen?

5. What was your communication partner's mood and did it affect performance?

6. What was my mood?

7. How good was the session?

8. What have I learned?

APPENDIX FOUR: EXAMPLE OF COMPLETED RECORD FORM TWO

INTERACTION DAILY RECORD

Interaction partners:

Date and time:

Place and situation:

1. Did your interaction partner enjoy the session and any parts of it in particular?
I would say she was certainly interested and she appeared to enjoy it more as it went on.

2. If not, when and why?
Several times at the beginning she showed annoyance - I was too keen and so too pushy I think.

3. How effective was the signalling today?
It took me a while to recognise 'back off' - it was better once I did!

4. Did anything new happen?
Towards the end she reached out and touched my face - brief eye contact too.

5. What was your communication partner's mood and did it affect performance?
Okay - it improved.

6. What was my mood?
I was a bit wound up to start with - think that's what made me too pushy.

7. How good was the session?
It came good after a faltering start - lots to build on for next time.

8. What have I learned?
How important it is to relax and sensitise myself to Julie. To slow down a bit and not worry so much about making something happen. She's getting to like faces more.

APPENDIX FIVE: SELF- APPRAISAL FORM FOR INTERACTIVE STYLE

The self-appraisal form contains a range of interaction styles from least sensitive to most sensitive, based on a parent coaching programme developed by Clark and Seifer (1983). It lends itself well to being used to evaluate your own interactive style as you begin Intensive Interaction or as you develop your abilities with the approach. You could use the form to reflect on your interactions as you think of them, or as you see them on video.

SELF-APPRAISAL FORM FOR INTERACTIVE STYLE

Am I regularly...

Uninvolved: mechanical in my interactions with little eye contact or smiling

Forcing: demanding in my interactions, eg turning the head of the person with SLD to make them look

Overriding: intrusive in my interactions, interrupting the flow of the person's activity with a requirement for a different behaviour or activity

Involved: responsive to the person's activity, experiencing enjoyment, perhaps expressed though eye contact and smiling

Acknowledging: responsive in a way that shows I've noticed the person's behaviour, animated in my facial expressions and verbal comment, attending and perhaps nodding

Imitating: responsive in a way that involves mirroring an aspect of the person's behaviour, vocalisation or facial expression

Expanding: responsive in a way that involves imitating an aspect of the person's behaviour, and adding a variation, or a verbal description, or questions, or linked behaviour

Elaborating: responsive in a way that involves commenting on the person's activities, interpreting their intent, and asking questions

Engaging: responsive in a way that builds on your knowledge of the person and of how to engage them for extended periods

---

REFERENCES

Beveridge, M., Conti-Ramsden, G. & Leudar, I. (1989) *Language and Communication in People with Learning Disabilities*. London: Routledge

Bullowa, M. (ed) (1979) *Before Speech*. Cambridge: Cambridge University Press.

Caldwell, P. (1996) *Getting in Touch: Ways of Working with People with Severe Learning Disabilities and Extensive Support Needs*. London: Pavillion.

Clark, G.N. & Seifer, R. (1983) 'Facilitating mother-infant communication: a treatment model for high-risk and developmentally delayed infants', Infant Mental Health Journal, 4, 2, 67-82.

Coupe O'Kane & B. Smith (eds) *Taking Control: Enabling People with Learning Difficulties*. London: David Fulton.

Coupe O'Kane, J. & Goldbart, J. (2nd edn) (1998) *Communication Before Speech: Development and Assessment*. London: David Fulton.

Field, T. (1979) 'Games parents play with normal and high-risk infants', Child Psychiatry and Human Development, 10, 1, 41-48.

Grove, N., Porter, J. & Park, K. 'Ages and Stages: What is Appropriate Behaviour?' in J. Coupe O'Kane & J. Goldbart (eds) (1996) *Whose Choice? Contentious Issues for those Working with People with Learning Difficulties*. London: David Fulton.

Hewett, D. & Nind, M. 'Commentary one: practice and progress' in D. Hewett & M. Nind (eds) (1998) *Interaction in Action: Reflections on the Use of Intensive Interaction*. London: David Fulton.

Hewett, D. & Nind, M. (eds) (1998) *Interaction in Action: Reflections on the Use of Intensive Interaction*. London: David Fulton.

Hodapp, R.M. & Goldfield, E.C. (1983) 'The use of mother-infant games as therapy with delayed children', Early Child Development and Care, 13, 17-32

Lewis, M. & Rosenblum, R.A. (eds) (1974) *The Effect of the Infant on its Caregiver*. New York: Wiley

Lovell, Jones, & Ephraim, G. (1998) 'The effect of Intensive Interaction on the sociability of a man with severe intellectual disabilities', International Journal of Practical Approaches to Disability, 23, 2/3, 3-9.

Marsh, P. (1988) *Eye to Eye: How People Interact*. Oxford: Guild Publishing

McConkey, R. 'Interaction: the name of the game' in B. Smith (ed) (1987) *Interactive Approaches to the Education of Children with Severe Learning Difficulties*. Birmingham: Westhill College

Nind, M. (1996) 'Efficacy of Intensive Interaction', European Journal of Special Needs Education, 11, 48-66

Nind (1999) 'Intensive Interaction and autism: a useful approach?', British Journal of Special Education, 26, 2, 96-102

Nind, M. & Hewett, D. 'When age-appropriateness isn't appropriate' in J. Coupe O'Kane & J. Goldbart (eds) (1996) *Whose Choice? Contentious Issues for those Working with People with Learning Difficulties.* London: David Fulton.

Nind, M. & Hewett, D. (1994) *Access to Communication: Developing the Basics of Communication with People with Severe Learning Difficulties through Intensive Interaction.* London: David Fulton.

Schaffer, H.R. (1977) *Studies in Mother-Infant Interaction.* London: Academic Press

Schaffer, H.R. (1996) *Social Development.* London: Routledge

Smith, B. 'Discussion: Age-Appropriate or Developmentally Appropriate Activities?' in J. Coupe O'Kane & J. Goldbart (eds) (1996) *Whose Choice? Contentious Issues for those Working with People with Learning Difficulties.* London: David Fulton.

Watson, J. & Fisher, A. (1997) 'Evaluating the effectiveness of Intensive Interaction teaching with pupils with profound and complex learning difficulties', British Journal of Special Education, 24, 2, 80-87

Ware, J. (1996) *Creating a Responsive Environment for people with Profound and Multiple Learning Difficulties.* London: David Fulton.